© **1993 by Vernon A. Stone**
All rights reserved

Except for appropriate use in critical reviews or works of scholarship, the reproduction or use of this work in any form or by any electronic, mechanical or other means now known or hereafter invented, including photocopying and recording, and in any information storage and retrieval system is forbidden without the written permission of the publisher.

97 96 95 94 93   5 4 3 2 1

Library of Congress Catalog Card Number: 93-072159

International Standard Book Number: 1-56625-031-5

Bonus Books, Inc.
160 East Illinois Street
Chicago, Illinois 60611

Printed in the United States of America

To Hallie and Adam

Contents

Preface — vii

1. How Much? — 1
2. TV Averages — 13
3. Radio Averages — 31
4. Salary Ranges — 39
5. Salary Trends — 53
6. Minorities and Women — 69
7. Salary Satisfaction — 83
8. Overtime — 91
9. Interns — 99
10. Staff Benefits — 111
11. Bottom and Top — 125
12. Looking to 2000 — 137

Appendix A: Survey Materials — 151
Appendix B: TV Markets by ADI Categories — 161
Appendix C: Trends Tables for Middle Markets — 167
Notes — 175
Bibliography — 183
Index — 191

Preface

This book was written primarily for journalists and others in broadcasting. From beginning reporters to veteran anchors and general managers, they want to know what's being paid in the field. So do high school and college students considering broadcast news as a career, and their faculty advisers and career counselors. The book is also for fellow researchers, print reporters and possibly some listeners and viewers who would like to know more about the people who bring them the news.

The writer has been most of the above: TV and radio journalist, educator, adviser to many students, a researcher who has often treated research as a form of reporting, and a broadcast news consumer since childhood days when I imagined those men who "gave the news" on radio must make a lot of money.

The book draws on 20 years of survey research, much of it related to my serving as research director for the Radio-Television News Directors Association (RTNDA). Most of the findings have not been previously reported. Averages published annually in RTNDA's *Communicator* served only as a starting point for analyzing salaries and related variables for trends. The book takes the place of several articles that would be scattered across scholarly journals and a few years of publication lags.

Trends are at the heart of it all. Salary averages and distributions are reported in the context of changing times and comparable occupations. Past trends are analyzed further to show what salaries may look like in the future. Changes across the past two decades are used to help explain pay gaps by race and sex. Trends in overtime and staff benefits are reported, as are changes in the use of interns. Journalists tell how well their pay is meeting their needs and expectations. There are closeups of some of the field's lowest paid and highest paid. Finally, news directors join me in looking to the year 2000.

All I had intended to write on pay was a chapter or two in a book on past and future trends in TV and radio news operations. Then it became apparent that I had enough for a dozen chapters or so just on salaries and related topics. So the spinoff is coming first. The other book, in progress, will report research on such topics as staff size and diversity, hiring patterns, newsroom finances, budgetary cutbacks, the use of consultants, the role of cable and the changing news product.

Survey data for the present book were collected from 1972 to 1992 with the help of dozens of graduate and undergraduate research assistants, secretaries and other clerical workers at the Universities of Wisconsin, Georgia, Southern Illinois and Missouri. Missouri doctoral student assistant Wenbing Chen spent hundreds of hours remastering old data files, many originally on punch cards, for use in current computer systems. Graduate assistant Kim Burks coordinated the mailing, processing and coding of questionnaires in a careers survey of more than 2,100 TV and radio journalists. Help on various recent research came from student assistants Jack Hodgson, Shephali Joshi and Chris DeFilippis and secretaries Kathy Sharp and Janet Traxler Stewart. For 20 years, teams of three to five persons per year have typically helped with my surveys. Their names are too many to list, but their assistance is gratefully acknowledged.

Professor Mike McKean of Missouri read the full working manuscript and made helpful suggestions. Parts were read by broadcast journalists Karen Foss and Tony Villasana, KSDK-TV, St. Louis; Lee Giles, WISH-TV, Indianapolis; Lee Hall, WSB, Atlanta; Gary Hanson (1992-93 RTNDA chairman), WKBN-TV,

Youngstown, Ohio; Georgeann Herbert, WBBM, Chicago; and Emily Rooney, ABC News, New York. For their interest and perceptive comments, I am most grateful.

For any shortcomings in the book, I take full responsibility.

RTNDA deserves much credit. From 1972 through 1992, the surveys of news directors were supported in part by unrestricted grants from RTNDA as a service to the field. Suggestions from RTNDA officers, directors and members have helped keep the research attuned to the changing world of broadcast journalism. But final decisions and the research have always been left to me. For RTNDA's generous support, my deepest appreciation.

Thanks also go to the Freedom Forum for a grant that supported surveys in 1990-91 of television and radio journalists on their career progress and obstacles, with particular attention to minorities and women. Only findings related to salaries are included here. Others will be published later.

Finally, my thanks to the thousands of news directors and other broadcast journalists who have taken valuable time to respond to my surveys over the years. Without their cooperation, there would be no book.

CHAPTER 1

How Much?

How much can a radio news director expect to earn in a small market? On average, about $15,000 a year.

How much in a medium market (50,000–250,000 population)? $18,000.

How much for a TV news director in a small market? $31,000 in the 60 smallest, which are roughly the size of radio's medium markets.

How much does a small-market TV station pay a typical reporter? About $14,000, on average.

Seems low for someone with a college degree. How many small-market stations would more likely pay, let's say, $20,000? About 7 percent.

Looking ahead, based on change in the past five years, how much can a small-market TV reporter expect in the year 2000? Sorry, the average has been going down. If that doesn't change, $13,000 by 2000.

Anchors are said to make the best money. How have those small-market TV stations been paying their anchors? $20,000 for typical anchors in 1987. $20,000 in 1992. At that rate, it looks like $20,000 for 2000.

Then let's try larger markets. At one of the network affiliates in the 25 largest markets, how much does an average TV anchor make? $150,000 in 1992. And the prices keep going up—$335,000 projected for 2000.

How about the stars, the highest paid anchors at their stations? On average, at ADI 1-25 affiliates, $264,000 in 1992. And at the 1987-92 average annual growth rate, headed for a median $726,000 in 2000.

How much? How much? For years my phone has regularly brought that question—from news directors, producers, general managers, trade press reporters and students planning careers or writing term papers. Even if they have read the RTNDA *Communicator* report on my latest annual survey, they want to know more. Those articles are pretty sketchy, of course—just who's making what and where. For the bigger picture of past and future trends in TV and radio news salaries, further data analysis was needed.

Now that such work has been done for this book, some of the findings give reason for concern. For example: (1) The pay gap between most staff—reporters, photographers and producers—and the stars (anchors) and managers is widening. (2) So is the gap between big-time and small-time.

The additive effects yield extreme contrasts. Consider this: In 1982, a broadcast group would have had to lay off seven small-market TV reporters to pay for one star anchor in a major market. By 1992, it took 19 minor league journalists to pay for one major league star anchor. By 2000, if the gap keeps widening at the 1987-92 rate, the ratio will be 55 to 1. But the reporter in a market the size of Quincy still pays Illinois sales tax at the same rate as the star anchor in Chicago, and one may pay about as much as the other for medical care.

Let's assume that sky-high anchor salaries are justified in real life, as the Jack Nicholson character does in the movie "Broadcast News." That leaves the other extreme—TV newsrooms in small-markets and radio newsrooms in small, medium and large markets. Evidence reported in this book suggests that they are becoming salary disaster areas.

First, how the evidence, the salary data, came to be.

Survey Procedures

News Director Surveys

These started in 1972 with a call from Fred Heckman, the everlasting news director (still there in 1993) at WIBC, Indianapolis. As chairman of the RTNDA Research Committee, he needed a survey of the nation's news directors. I did one and RTNDA wanted more. By the late 1970s, my "RTNDA surveys" and *Communicator* reports had become an annual project.

From the start of these multi-topic surveys, the topic of most interest to broadcasters has been pay. Readers let this be known when salaries were omitted from the 1973 surveys.

So salary items went back on to stay. They come at the end of the questionnaire, the best location for topics that may be sensitive or highly confidential. Some stations have rules against disclosing salaries, but the respondents most often fill in the requested salary numbers. Perhaps because the "salary surveys" have gained so many followers, the cooperation rate for pay items has gone up in recent years, as detailed in Table 1.1. In 1992, only 9 percent of the responding TV news directors and 27 percent of the ones in radio left the salary section blank.

TV and radio questionnaires and the cover letter mailed in the 1992 RTNDA-sponsored survey are included in Appendix A.

Survey items on salaries have evolved with the industry over the years. Weekly pay has given way to the annual numbers by which salaries are now commonly expressed. Items for high and low staff pay were dropped when specific positions were found to yield roughly the same information. It turns out that a newsroom's top pay usually goes to the news director in small and medium markets and to an anchor in the majors. A photographer is at the bottom in most cases. Two early items, "inexperienced beginner" and "five-year veteran," were dropped because pay for such staff depends on the position.

Rather than check salary categories as in many surveys, respondents write in salary amounts. This enhances precision.

TABLE 1.1: Survey Response Rates 1972–92

TV	Usable Q-aires	% of Mailing	News Ops	Telling Salaries	% of Ops
1972	406	64.3	398	264	66.3
1976	415	64.3	405	310	76.5
1977	432	68.0	428	328	76.6
1979	473	70.6	466	344	73.8
1980	495	72.8	484	350	72.3
1981	448	64.9	444	307	69.1
1982	450	65.2	446	307	68.8
1983	432	62.6	421	285	67.7
1984	463	63.9	445	282	63.4
1985	453	60.4	427	309	72.4
1986	435	58.0	396	254	64.1
1987	375	44.1	334	290	86.8
1988	459	51.6	382	319	83.5
1989	493	51.9	384	330	85.9
1990	554	57.7	447	385	86.1
1991	506	52.7	412	353	85.7
1992	525	54.7	419	381	90.9
Radio					
1972	346	44.9	343	193	56.3
1976	330	42.0	314	192	61.1
1977	458	48.7	444	292	65.8
1979	400	48.2	386	231	59.8
1980	389	46.6	377	265	70.2
1981	356	44.2	344	245	71.2
1982	350	42.9	341	219	64.2
1983	371	45.5	354	217	61.3
1984	327	39.6	319	173	54.2
1985	403	47.4	388	230	59.3
1986	405	47.6	390	203	52.1
1987	355	42.8	341	265	77.7
1988	373	45.2	337	269	79.8
1989	352	42.9	324	247	76.2
1990	384	46.8	350	268	76.6
1991	315	38.9	275	214	77.8
1992	343	41.8	296	217	73.3

Steps in the surveys have remained pretty much the same across the years. Questionnaires are mailed in May or June to news directors at all non-satellite commercial TV stations and a systematic random sample of commercial radio stations with working addresses in the year's *Broadcasting Yearbook* (succeeded in 1992 by Bowker's *Broadcasting & Cable Market Place*). When the yearbook indicates that jointly owned AM and FM stations have only one news operation, only one station is selected. Radio sampling is at a rate chosen to bring enough responses for reliable analysis of subsamples, which are fewer in radio than in television. The sampling rate has evolved from one of every six potential radio news operations in the 1970s to one of eight in the 1980s and 1990s.

To assure that a second mailing goes only to non-respondents, survey forms in the first mailing go out with call letters and cities filled in. Confidentiality is assured in the cover letter.

In the second mailing to non-respondents six to eight weeks later, identification is left blank on the survey forms, but most respondents choose to identify their stations by filling in the ID blanks.

TV news survey forms get thrown out more often than in the early years before everyone got into the act of surveying TV news directors. It has become the thing to do for a master's thesis or a faculty member's grind toward tenure. In major markets, filling out all of them could require an assistant news director for surveys. A few shops simplify matters by giving equal wastebasket treatment to all surveys, good or bad. As Table 1.1 shows, cooperation rates for my RTNDA-sponsored surveys of TV newsrooms has eroded from about two-thirds in the 1970s to just over half in the 1990s.

In radio, where return rates are always lower, there's been little change—42-48 percent most years, with no trend over time.

Bulk mailing and business reply envelopes have been used since the late 1970s. Response rates were no better for the hand-stamped first-class mail used earlier.

Addressing is to the generic "News Director." That's easier than using names, which are often unavailable. Better, too. The mailing doesn't get forwarded to a long gone ND. And in these days of personalized letters from sweepstakes maestro Ed McMahon and others, personal addressing means little.

News Staff Careers Survey

Salary data for this book also came from a survey of samples of all broadcast journalists conducted in 1990-91 under a grant from the Freedom Forum. The study was designed to compare minorities, women and white men on career goals, progress, obstacles and satisfaction as related to numerous variables including pay. Complete findings will be reported in a later book. The four-page TV questionnaire is included in Appendix A. The radio version does not differ substantively.

The careers survey took the two-stage approach of using news directors to distribute questionnaires and business reply envelopes to all their news staff, including themselves.

In television, the object was to get survey packets to about 4,900 news staff at a sample of 163 stations whose news directors had been contacted by phone and had promised to cooperate. Stations were chosen at random from 384 that had responded in the 1989 RTNDA-sponsored survey of news directors. Approximate staff sizes were known from the earlier survey. Turndowns came from 24 other NDs, leaving a cooperation rate of 87 percent for that stage. In the final stage, 1,781 staff returned questionnaires, 36 percent of all that were distributed to newsrooms.

The radio careers survey, conducted in two waves in 1991, was intended for 2,000 staff in the 625 news operations that returned questionnaires in RTNDA-sponsored surveys in 1990 and 1991, for which different sample frames were used. Questionnaires were completed by 414 radio news staff, 21 percent of the intended. Radio's low rate was not unexpected. The appeal to news directors was by mail with no prior phone request for cooperation. It's assumed that many of the 2,000 survey packets were thrown out along the way. Also, 40 percent of radio staff worked in news only part-time and may have been less likely than TV's full-timers to relate to the survey.

The staff careers survey, like the surveys of news directors, went only to TV and radio stations, not to networks. Any references to network news salaries draw upon secondary sources.

> Keep in mind throughout this book draws upon two kinds of surveys with different objectives: (1) RTNDA-sponsored surveys of news directors—to find what average stations are paying; (2) the Freedom Forum-sponsored careers survey of staff—to find what average staff are making. Within categories of market size, the two usually give about the same results.
>
> All tables are from the RTNDA-sponsored surveys, except in Chapters 6 (minorities and women), 7 (salary satisfaction), 9 (interns) and 11 (bottom and top earners).
>
> Newsroom managers, the primary readers of the RTNDA-sponsored survey reports, want to know what the average station is paying. Rank and file journalists want that, too. But they also want work force figures of the kind gathered in the careers survey sponsored by Freedom-Forum. When findings from the two types of surveys differ notably, that's reported.

Market Size

TV markets are ranked by Arbitron's ADI (Area of Dominant Influence) listings by the number of TV households in a market. The 210 ADI's for 1991-92, ranging from New York City to Alpena, Michigan, are listed in Appendix B.

Radio stations are categorized by market population: more than 1-million, major; 250,000-1,000,000, large; 50,000-250,000, medium; and less than 50,000, small. Arbitron's listings for radio are limited mainly to markets of 100,000 or more. To accommodate stations in smaller markets as well, I developed my own categories in 1972.

TV stations are seldom found in markets smaller than 50,000. The smallest market category for television, ADI 151-210, is roughly comparable to "medium" for radio. ADI 51-150 includes most of radio's "large" markets. TV's ADI 1-50 markets have populations of at least a million, as do "major" markets in radio.

ADI 1-25 TV stations include the great majority of independents that have news operations. Network affiliates are defined here as stations with ABC, CBS or NBC. Stations carrying the emerging Fox network are treated as independents for comparability across surveys.

Staff Size

The larger the TV market, the larger the average news staff (Table 1.2), at least for ABC, CBS and NBC affiliates. At independent stations with news staffs, most are small, even in the largest markets. If salaries for affiliates and indies in ADI 1-25 are not computed separately, the results are spuriously low. Outside the top 25 markets, indies with news operations are so few that including them makes little difference.

TABLE 1.2: News Staff Size—1992

	Full-Time		Including Part-Time		
	Median	Mean	Median	Mean	N
All TV	22.3	28.6	25.4	32.2	419
Net Affiliates	23.7	30.2	27.6	33.8	362
Independents	12.6	18.3	15.8	22.6	57
ADI 1-25 Affils	79.0	82.2	86.5	88.3	40
ADI 1-25 Indies	14.5	21.9	16.4	26.8	36
ADI 26-50	44.4	41.4	49.0	45.8	56
ADI 51-100	27.6	25.9	31.2	29.2	114
ADI 101-150	18.2	18.0	21.2	20.8	100
ADI 151-210	12.8	13.2	15.1	16.3	66
All Radio	1.0	1.5	2.0	2.7	296
Major Markets	1.2	2.9	2.4	4.2	39
Large Markets	1.2	1.8	1.8	3.0	55
Medium Markets	1.1	1.2	2.0	2.5	97
Small Markets	.9	1.1	2.0	2.3	105

News staff size at average radio stations differs little by market size. Staffs of more than three full-time newspeople are seldom found outside major markets. And whether a market has more than a million population or less than 50,000, its average station has only one full-time and one part-time newsperson.

U. S. Areas

Regional breaks are by East, South, Midwest and West, according to U.S. Census Bureau classifications which have been used in these surveys since 1972.[1]

Buying Power

For most people, money matters only for what it can buy. Salary changes across time take on meaning when compared to changes in the cost of living. For years, my salary research has related pay to the Consumer Price Index for all Urban Consumers. The CPI-U, the standard source from the Bureau of Labor Statistics of the U.S. Department of Labor, is said to represent the buying habits of about 80 percent of the non-institutional population. The index is used to measure average change in the prices paid by consumers for a fixed market basket of goods and services. These include food, clothing, shelter, fuel, drugs, transportation, medical bills and other goods and services that people buy for day-to-day living, plus sales and use taxes.

As noted earlier, the Illinois sales tax rate is the same for a reporter in Quincy and a star anchor in Chicago. While the cost of living is less in Quincy, that difference is nowhere near the gap between the TV news pay scales in the two markets. The trade-off for a small market's low cost of living is often a low salary ceiling.

Staff Benefits

If you must pay for part or all of your health insurance, as is increasingly the case, there goes a big hunk of your salary. Nothing else in the CPI's market basket has gone up like medical care, especially if it comes in a hospital. Medical and dental insurance and other staff benefits are important parts of the total compensation package. A special survey looked at what stations were providing their staff in health insurance for themselves and dependents, life insurance, contributions to pension plans, profit-sharing and bonuses. The cost of those benefits figures into a salary's net worth and the newsperson's buying power.

Staff who can least afford it are the ones most likely to be left to shift for themselves on medical costs, etc. Newspeople in large markets enjoy the best benefits packages as well as salaries. TV reporters or radio news directors in small markets often have to take those costs out of paychecks that may already approach poverty level.

Though not a staff benefit as such, overtime availability also makes a difference in that all-important buying power. A few hours extra at time-and-a-half can make the difference between just getting by and doing so in style. But overtime is less often available than in the old days. Now there's "comp time" or job categories that carry 50-60 hours a week at a flat "salary" because you're a "professional."

Research by Others

Published accounts of broadcast news salaries have tended toward the anecdotal, mostly stories on million-dollar anchors. Low paid reporters and producers make dull copy.

One of the earliest of the few systematic studies was by Irving E. Fang and Frank W. Gerval at the University of Minnesota. Their national survey of commercial TV newsrooms in 1970 found median salaries of about $6,800 for beginners and $9,600 for five-year veterans. They did not report pay by position.[2]

Salary data also came from a 1970 survey by John W. C. Johnstone, Edward J. Slawski and William W. Bowman, sociologists at the University of Illinois at Chicago. They found median pay of $11,875 for TV and $9,585 for radio news. The survey included newspeople at daily and weekly newspapers, news magazines and wire services, as well. Subsamples for radio and television were too small to break out by staff positions.[3]

Two similar follow-up surveys of American journalists have been conducted by David H. Weaver and G. Cleveland Wilhoit at Indiana University. In 1981, they found medians of $17,030 for TV and $15,000 for radio news staff.[4] In 1991, their survey found $25,625 for television and $20,355 for radio. Subsamples of 138 for television and 101 for radio in 1991 were not further analyzed by staff position.[5]

Conrad Smith, Eric Fredin and Carroll Ann Ferguson at Ohio State University surveyed TV reporters in 1986 and found medians of $20,020 for women and $24,440 for men.[6] More than a third of the reporters surveyed were in the 50 largest markets.

For two decades, Kenneth Harwood of the University of Houston has been analyzing and reporting broadcast earnings data compiled by the Bureau of Labor Statistics and other agencies of the U. S. government.[7] His comparisons with other occupations have been particularly useful.

For several years, Lee Becker and colleagues at Ohio State have worked with Tom Engleman of the Dow Jones Newspaper Fund to survey entry-level pay of recent journalism graduates in all major specialties. Newspapers, advertising and public relations all offer higher starting salaries than TV or radio news.[8]

Besides mine, the only surveys across both years and positions are the bi-annual ones by the National Association of Broadcasters.[9] The NAB surveys, covering the whole station, also gather information on staff benefits. The NAB surveys complement mine by enabling comparisons outside the newsroom. For example, not only do TV anchors in the largest markets earn more than their news directors, as I have long found. NAB numbers show that major-market anchors also out-earn their stations' general managers.

CHAPTER 2

TV Averages

Averages can be tickets to mediocrity. After all, who wants to be just average? Where pay is concerned, lots of television stations do. They want ratings that are above average, but staff who work cheap. To stay respectably average, they check the medians from salary surveys.

My latest survey found that the majority of TV news staff failed to keep up with the cost of living from mid-1991 to mid-1992. The Consumer Price Index rose 3.1 percent in the 12 months, its smallest increase in six years. But rank and file anchors, reporters and photographers—whose combined numbers make up two-thirds of all news staff—saw their median salaries go up less than the CPI. Producers, news directors and other newsroom managers outpaced the CPI overall, but mainly in the 50 largest markets. TV anchors in the largest operations beat inflation handily, as usual.[1]

As context for looking at broadcast news salaries, let's keep in mind that a 1990 Census Bureau survey found a median of $25,392 for workers whose highest education was a bachelor's degree, as is the case for most in TV and radio news.[2] To estimate roughly for 1992, add $1,000 or so.

Why the median? That's the typical salary, what the average person makes, the one in the middle. The mean, on the other hand, is the average of all salaries—the sum divided by the number of cases. Its problem is that a few extreme cases can distort the mean away from what the average person earns. Extremes have little if any effect on the median.[3]

But extremes may also be part of the story. Means, alongside medians as in this chapter's tables, can cue us to big highs or little lows that skew the distribution of salaries. The mean and median are identical in the rare perfectly normal distribution. If the mean is much larger than the median, a few stations are paying far more than most. If it's much smaller, watch out for sweatshops.

TV news staff fall into three overlapping categories:

1. Basic journalists, the creators of the news product, the great majority of staff. Photographers and reporters get the stories with audio and video. Assignment editors are central in deciding what gets covered. Producers turn it all into news programs.
2. Anchors, who may also get out and do reporting, are the program stars, with reporters as the supporting cast.
3. Newsroom managers. News directors, assistant news directors, managing editors and executive producers coordinate, supervise and make decisions.

Basic Journalists

Let's start at the salary bottom and move up.

Photographers

Whether they're called photojournalists, videographers or shooters, the operators of electronic news gathering (ENG) cameras are at the heart of TV news. It's their eye on the world that distinguishes television from other news media. Yet, photographers are usually the lowest paid news staff. The median station in 1992 paid typical photographers about $18,000.

TABLE 2.1: Typical TV News Photographers

	Median	Mean	N
All Stations	$18,120	$21,530	356
Network Affiliates	17,885	21,120	316
Independents	21,300	24,760	40
ADI 1-25 Affils	38,500	41,125	39
ADI 1-25 Indies	29,375	28,630	25
ADI 26-50	24,575	24,500	51
ADI 51-100	18,475	18,710	102
ADI 101-150	15,675	15,975	86
ADI 151-210	13,055	13,780	47
East	21,350	25,525	50
South	17,260	18,940	120
Midwest	18,750	20,985	104
West	18,750	23,580	82

As it does for other staff, pay for photographers goes up with market size. In small and middle markets, differences are not great—averages are in the teens, with medians and means that look much alike. In short, few stations stand out—most pay low. Salaries go up substantially, by about $6,000, with a move to the ADI 1-25 market category. But the big jump, by another $15,000 or so, comes when photographers move to network affiliates in the 25 largest markets. In major markets, they are most often unionized.

Independent stations, overall, have higher averages than network affiliates, but only because most indie newsrooms are found in large markets. Within ADI 1-25, photographers—and other staff—earn more at affiliates, which typically invest much more in their news operations.

External comparisons also show TV news photographers at the bottom. Commercial photographers averaged about $24,800 and government photographers $29,200 in 1991. Daily newspaper photographers in 1992 had medians of $21,860 in small markets, $33,950 in medium and $52,975 in major markets (circulation of more than 500,000). Even TV photojournalists in major markets earn much less than their counterparts in print.[4]

Their salaries are higher in the East than elsewhere. That tends to be the case for most TV news positions, because of the concentration of major markets. Means are much higher than medians in both the East and West, boosted by union shops in markets like New York and Los Angeles.

Well over half of the photojournalists responding in the separate careers survey were from top-50 markets. Not surprisingly, their overall median was a much higher $28,450. The mean was $28,400. Averages within market categories were similar to the ones from the news directors survey.

The average TV station is paying its photojournalists as neither photographers nor journalists. Their median pay is closer to that of the $19,240 being paid the average busdriver in the early 1990s.

Reporters

The median station pays its typical reporters only about $2,000 more than photographers. Indeed, the reporter and photographer are the same person in small, one-person-band shops. Among ADI survey respondents, 61 listed salaries for reporters but only 47 for photographers. ENG photography is just double-duty for reporters at some of those stations. The mean of roughly $25,900 for reporters overwhelms the median of $20,100 because pay is much higher in large markets than in small or middle ones. The median station normally falls in a middle market.

Hard times are no stranger to reporters in the 60 smallest

TV markets. Their median for 1992 was slightly below the federal government's official 1991 poverty level of $13,924 for a famliy of four.[5]

To do better than averages under $20,000, reporters must move to a middle market, where the low 20s prevail. Moving to ADI 26-50 adds an average of $10,000. At the next stop, an ADI 1-25 network affiliate, add another $25,000 or so. That's where the years of paying dues pays off.

TABLE 2.2: Typical TV Reporters

	Median	Mean	N
All Stations	$20,130	$25,915	381
Network Affiliates	19,895	25,405	340
Independents	24,750	30,150	41
ADI 1-25 Affils	55,500	61,310	39
ADI 1-25 Indies	31,250	36,295	24
ADI 26-50	30,615	31,505	51
ADI 51-100	20,500	21,565	106
ADI 101-150	16,900	17,285	93
ADI 151-210	13,845	14,535	61
East	27,750	32,975	52
South	19,750	23,065	126
Midwest	19,360	24,930	112
West	20,940	27,045	91

And openings will come. Stations in the 50 largest markets employ about half of the nation's TV reporters, as indicated by the 1990-91 careers survey. Reporters showed a median of $28,000 and mean of $36,200 in that study sampling people instead of stations.

In the 1992 survey of stations, the median for TV reporters in ADI 1-25 news operations was roughly the same as the $56,000 earned by senior reporters (five-plus years in news) at daily newspapers in major markets. But in small and middle markets, TV reporters averaged several thousand dollars less than their print counterparts. Daily newspaper reporters with one to four years' experience had 1992 medians of about $21,000 at small-circulation dailies and $26,500 at medium-circulation dailies.

TV reporters average less than producers in small and middle markets, but more in ADI 1-50. The floor is low but the ceiling higher for reporters and anchors. When you make the big time on camera, money comes your way.

Salaries for TV reporters are highest in the East. Also, as for photographers, means are much higher than medians in the East and West, where unionization in major markets is most often found.

The typical TV reporter's pay is nowhere near the national median of $33,700 for high school teachers. It's closer to the median salaries for computer operators ($19,350) and licensed practical nurses ($19,400). Peanut roasters in Georgia average more ($21,700).

Producers

On average, stations pay typical producers just over $22,000, a couple of thousand more than reporters. But there's less gain for producers when they move up. Even the median ADI 1-25 affiliate logs in at no more than $40,000 for average producers, and that's $15,000 less than reporters make in those markets. In the 50 largest markets, reporters not only overtake producers, they leave them behind.

Still, the pay is clearly best in the big operations, and they're the ones that employ several producers each. Some small operations have no producers as such. Only half of the responding stations in ADI 151-210 listed pay for producers. In the careers survey, with nearly half of the responding producers in the 25 largest markets, the median for all markets combined was $26,300 and the mean was $30,900. Within market-size categories, averages from the two types of surveys differed little.

TABLE 2.3: Typical TV News Producers

	Median	Mean	N
All Stations	$22,145	$24,760	313
Network Affiliates	21,900	24,225	280
Independents	25,000	29,280	33
ADI 1-25 Affils	39,915	42,290	38
ADI 1-25 Indies	28,750	32,895	22
ADI 26-50	28,500	28,150	50
ADI 51-100	21,250	21,650	92
ADI 101-150	17,800	18,635	73
ADI 151-210	14,930	15,675	32
East	24,750	27,525	44
South	20,750	22,175	104
Midwest	22,035	24,155	91
West	23,700	27,490	74

Compared to daily newspaper staff, producers' pay is closest to that of copy editors with up to four years of experience whose medians were $21,320 in small, $28,650 in medium and $41,590 in major markets.

Assignment Editors

Starting lower than producers but peaking at about the same level at ADI 1-25 affiliates, assignment editors were found to earn just over $28,000, on average. Extremes are rare, and the mean is not much greater than the median. Regional differences are minor.

Assistant city editors, probably the most comparable staff at daily newspapers, average $28,300 in small, $38,400 in medium and $59,200 in major markets—at each level, several thousand dollars more than TV assignment editors.

The typical assignment editor would earn a little more as a dental hygienist ($29,000) and a little less as manager of a small hotel or motel ($25,000).

TABLE 2.4: TV Assignment Editors

	Median	Mean	N
All Stations	$28,150	$29,180	300
Network Affiliates	28,020	29,995	269
Independents	28,750	30,770	31
ADI 1-25 Affils	39,875	42,525	39
ADI 1-25 Indies	32,750	34,040	20
ADI 26-50	34,000	33,760	48
ADI 51-100	28,035	28,480	88
ADI 101-150	21,875	21,615	66
ADI 151-210	17,875	19,795	34
East	29,150	31,825	43
South	27,000	28,290	98
Midwest	28,200	28,045	91
West	28,500	30,300	68

Anchors

Larger markets mean much larger paychecks for anchors, the persons most closely tied to ratings. In major markets, where ratings points translate to megabucks, the sky's the limit for anchors who can deliver. In small markets, the rewards are modest.

Typical Anchors

In Table 2.5, we see the mean of $54,630 running a good 19 lengths ahead of the median of $35,100. The median is far behind because the vast majority of stations are in small and middle markets where most anchors make well under $40,000. Triple that to get the anchor you want at a typical network affiliate in the 25 largest markets.

TABLE 2.5: Typical TV Anchors

	Median	Mean	N
All Stations	$35,100	$54,630	369
Network Affiliates	35,395	54,600	330
Independents	39,375	54,920	39
ADI 1-25 Affils	149,585	165,255	39
ADI 1-25 Indies	55,000	70,805	23
ADI 26-50	70,810	75,310	49
ADI 51-100	39,715	41,580	102
ADI 101-150	27,450	28,600	89
ADI 151-210	19,800	20,920	61
East	36,250	71,645	50
South	37,625	50,250	121
Midwest	35,375	47,950	111
West	34,750	59,475	87

Average independent stations in ADI 1-25 pay only about a third as much for anchors as do the network affiliates.

The average ADI 1-25 affiliate pays rank and file anchors seven to eight times as much as do ADI 151-210 stations.

Regionally, there's little difference in medians. But the means for typical anchors are highest in the East and West, thanks to supersalaries for stars in major markets, most notably New York and Los Angeles.

Anchors responding in the careers survey had a median salary of $37,875 and a mean of $64,920. Those results are similar to the ones from asking stations what they paid their typical anchors. That's because the responding anchors came in good numbers from markets of all sizes. Stations in small markets may get along without photographers, producers and even reporters. But they still must have at least two or three anchors.

TV anchors have no counterpart at daily newspapers. Comparable national salary medians are reported for stockbrokers ($36,000) and high school teachers ($37,700).

Star Anchors

It's an understatement to say that all anchors are not created equal, or so paid. The station's highest paid anchor normally goes to the bank with much more than others at the station. The larger the market, the larger the gap. So we have a mean of roughly $90,000, not far from twice the median of $50,000 for star anchors.

Again, the median is low because it falls in a middle market, where "star" anchors are had easily for, say, $50,000 or $60,000. But move into the top 50 markets and we're talking six digits. Get up around the top 10 and the highest paid will most often take in a quarter-million or more.

Big time vs. small time finds affiliates in the top 25 markets paying star anchors 10 times as much as stations in the bottom 60. An anchor in St. Joseph, Missouri, may work two weeks to earn as much as one in New York makes in one day. That's incentive to move up.

Stations in the East typically paid the most for their stars.

TABLE 2.6: Typical TV Station's Highest Paid Anchor

	Median	Mean	N
All Stations	$50,535	$90,375	335
Network Affiliates	53,250	92,455	299
Independents	49,000	73,075	36
ADI 1-25 Affils	263,750	330,930	35
ADI 1-25 Indies	62,500	90,710	24
ADI 26-50	118,335	121,425	40
ADI 51-100	58,250	65,290	93
ADI 101-150	35,400	38,935	85
ADI 151-210	26,625	29,945	53
East	70,000	142,035	45
South	53,625	77,390	113
Midwest	48,250	77,285	101
West	47,500	96,480	76

Around the Anchor Desk

Of the three or four people in the typical TV anchor team, who earns the most? The news anchor. Least? The sport anchor. In between is the weathercaster.

That's from a 1990 survey, my only one to assess salaries of sports anchors and weathercasters along with news anchors. Sports and weather specialists are part of the news staff at nine out of 10 stations. On average, the news anchor earns $2,000 more than the weathercaster, who's $3,000 ahead of the sports anchor.

At network affiliates in the 25 largest markets, medians for sports and weather talent are roughly the same, both well under the means. Again, that's because some major-market stations pay super salaries to all kinds of anchors. The medians and means look much alike in other market categories.

Two people do sports at the typical station. Averages are four to five at ADI 1-25 affiliate, three in ADI 26-50, two to three in 51-100, two in 101-151 and one to two in 151-210.

The typical station has two weather specialists. The average is three at ADI 1-50 affiliates and one in ADI 151-210.

TABLE 2.7: Median TV News Anchor Team Pay (1990)

	News	Weather	Sports	N
All TV	$35,000	$33,000	$30,000	373
ADI 1-25 Affils	120,835	100,750	100,400	35
ADI 1-25 Indies	50,000	49,750	45,000	24
ADI 26-50	59,750	53,500	45,000	48
ADI 51-100	39,905	35,035	34,900	111
ADI 101-150	27,900	26,000	23,000	89
ADI 151-210	21,610	19,900	20,400	66
East	33,800	35,000	32,500	62
South	35,090	34,955	30,020	122
Midwest	34,000	30,010	29,975	109
West	35,000	29,875	29,950	78

Half of the TV weatherpeople are trained meteorologists. The federal government paid average meteorologists $44,700 in 1991. Television comes up to that average only in the 50 largest markets.

Newsroom Managers

News directors, assistant news directors, managing editors and executive producers make most of a TV newsroom's managerial decisions. For this, all newsroom managers responding in 1991 to the careers survey earned a median of $41,930 and a mean of $49,930. Those averages are similar to the composite of the ones reported here from the 1992 survey of all TV stations.

Executive Producers

Only about half the stations outside the top 50 markets reported salaries for executive producers. Small shops often do without this position. The overall median of just over $35,000 falls between the ones for ADI 26-50 and 51-100. In all market categories, the mean is not much larger than the median. The gain from a lateral move tends to be small.

To move up, go east or west. Largely as an artifact of locations in megalopolises, stations in the East and West pay executive producers more than do those in the South and Midwest.

Comparable national medians are found for experienced (five-plus years) copy editors ($34,060) and senior (five-plus) reporters ($35,150) at daily newspapers in middle markets.

Outside the mass media in the early 1990s, the average architect earned $36,100 and the average editor for a book publisher, $33,000.

TABLE 2.8: TV Executive Producers

	Median	Mean	N
All Stations	$35,105	$38,865	194
Network Affiliates	35,000	38,535	175
Independents	37,500	41,930	19
ADI 1-25 Affils	64,285	65,365	33
ADI 1-25 Indies	42,500	45,605	16
ADI 26-50	41,565	42,205	39
ADI 51-100	32,375	32,510	51
ADI 101-150	21,875	24,265	35
ADI 151-210	19,500	22,315	16
East	39,000	44,250	28
South	33,500	34,700	71
Midwest	34,800	38,050	56
West	40,750	43,760	39

Assistant News Directors

TABLE 2.9: TV Assistant News Directors

	Median	Mean	N
All Stations	$41,000	$45,865	128
Network Affiliates	40,745	45,760	120
Independents	47,000	47,425	8
ADI 1-25 Affils	81,430	75,665	27
ADI 1-25 Indies	56,500	55,900	6
ADI 26-50	50,310	51,715	21
ADI 51-100	35,165	37,980	34
ADI 101-150	27,875	28,435	23
ADI 151-210	24,375	25,265	15
East	66,250	68,220	11
South	35,150	39,800	50
Midwest	44,875	43,810	37
West	42,500	50,315	30

Only about a third of the TV stations reported salaries for assistant news directors. Many newsrooms, especially smaller ones, have no such position. An assignment editor or executive producer is second in command. The national median of $41,000 for assistant news directors is about midway between the ones for news directors and executive producers. At ADI 1-25 affiliates, the median is less than the mean, indicating low pay for the position in a few of those big operations.

News Directors

On average, the news director is the highest paid person in the newsroom. That's for all but the 50 largest markets, where the star anchor typically makes the most. The median of $47,250 for news directors does not differ greatly from their mean of about $54,500.

TABLE 2.10: TV News Directors

	Median	Mean	N
All Stations	$47,250	$54,455	368
Network Affiliates	47,440	54,620	323
Independents	43,375	53,275	45
ADI 1-25 Affils	107,500	112,485	36
ADI 1-25 Indies	52,915	60,445	28
ADI 26-50	73,250	68,380	48
ADI 51-100	51,470	51,655	99
ADI 101-150	37,475	37,310	89
ADI 151-210	30,880	35,515	61
East	50,810	62,505	51
South	49,835	54,430	119
Midwest	44,250	50,500	111
West	44,335	54,810	87

News directors definitely better themselves financially by moving up. Gains by market size are progressive—roughly $7,000 for the typical move from ADI 151-210 to 101-150, $14,000 from there to 51-100, $21,000 in going on up to 26-50 and another $34,000 for the big move to an ADI 1-25 affiliate.

Regionally, the average news director earns more in the East or South than in the West or Midwest. The Midwest has a lot of low-paying markets.

The TV news director's daily newspaper counterpart, the managing editor, earns a few thousand dollars more. Medians for managing editors in 1992 were $39,360 at small-, $70,000 at middle- and $139,800 at major-circulation dailies.

News directors' salaries approximate those of public relations practitioners, who average in the 40s nationally. PR medians for 1990 were $44,400 in media relations and $49,100 in public affairs.

Entry Level

It may be a lean year—that first year out of school on your first job in TV news. On average, the pay in 1991 was between $14,000 and $15,000. Lee Becker and Gerald Kosicki of Ohio State, in a cross-media survey of a sample of journalism and mass communication graduates who had been out of school six to eight months, found a $14,455 median for 60 TV news staff.[6] Similarly, in my survey of TV journalists of all college majors the same year, those who had been out of school only one full year or less (N = 99) had a median of $14,855.

An NAB survey in 1991 reported mean starting salaries of $12,150 for TV photographers, $13,320 for reporters and $15,585 for producers in the 60 smallest markets.[7] (Means and medians tend to differ little at this level.) Average starting pay is not much higher in ADI 126-150 markets, but it jumps by about $2,000 with a move to ADI 101-125. As markets get larger, starting salaries apply more often to hires from other stations and less often to entry-level staff. NAB's best approximation of entry-level pay is probably the starting figures in ADI 125-210.

Contrary to conventional wisdom, new graduates get entry-level jobs in major markets as well as small markets and those between. My career survey's 99 journalists who had been out of school only a full year or less were distributed roughly a fourth each in ADI 1-50, 51-100, 101-150 and 151-210 markets. Entry-level writers, desk assistants and production assistants in major markets are normally paid more than the poverty wages going to the small-market reporters who are hired fresh from the classroom.

TV and radio news trail other media in entry-level pay. Becker and Kosicki found medians of $15,030 for weekly newspapers, $18,095 for advertising agencies and departments, $18,200 for daily newspapers and $20,020 for public relations.[8] Note that even county seat weeklies pay newcomers better than TV news.

But after that first year of on-the-job experience, TV news salaries tend to look a lot better. In my 1991 survey of TV journalists, the 103 with two years out of school logged in with a median of $16,825, almost $2,000 more than the ones in their first year. And many years later? Well, we've seen what major-league anchors make. Starting pay is lower in TV news than in print, but the ceiling for stars is higher.

Elsewhere at the TV Station

Few employees at the average station earn more than its news director and anchors. The 1991 NAB survey found higher medians only for the general manager ($100,000), general sales manager ($85,000) and assistant GM/station manager ($63,000). The NAB medians for news directors ($48,720) and anchors ($41,000) were moderately higher than the ones from my survey.[9]

Average anchors at network affiliates in the 10 largest markets, but only there, typically outearn their general manager ($208,230 vs. $190,000), according to the NAB survey.

The station's highest paid anchor (one of the salaries included in my survey reports but not NAB's) makes more than his or her general manager all the way down through the ADI 26-50 market category. In middle and small markets, the GM out-earns all anchors as well as all others.

The larger the market, the more the news director is valued relative to other managers. The news director's pay goes up more sharply with market size than does theirs. News directors at ADI 1-25 affiliates average three times as much as the ones in ADI 151-210. By comparison, GMs in the largest operations make just two and a half times as much as those in the smallest. General sales managers only double their pay by moving from bottom to top.

The general sales manager is typically the top paid department head in all market categories. The news director is second. The 1991 NAB survey found medians of $44,720 for chief engineers, $40,000 for operations managers and $38,000 for program directors. In TV's early days, when most stations did local programming in addition to news, program directors tended to earn more than news directors. But in the 1990s, program managers lag behind newsroom managers in markets of all sizes. A station's operations manager earns less than its news director in ADI 1-100 and more in 101-210. The chief engineer's pay is typically less than the news director's in ADI 1-100, but they make about the same in 101-210. The news director typically is paid as well as the assistant GM/station manager at ADI 1-25 network affiliates, but makes less in all other market categories.

On the low side, we have seen that photographers tend to get the smallest paychecks of all news staff. Elsewhere at the station, they average more than tape editors, staff artists, floor directors, traffic/computer operators and production assistants. That's for total stations surveyed by NAB and applies down through many middle-market stations. But relative pay gets worse for ENG camerapeople as markets get smaller. In the bottom tier (ADI 151-210), news photographers show up as the lowest paid of all "support staff" whose salaries are surveyed by NAB.

Technology may be a major player in the devaluation of photographers. Newsfilm, and even early ENG, required more technical skill than do today's highly automated video cameras. After all, millions of Americans now use camcorders. Stations may be finding they can get video that does the job without the cost of highly trained or experienced photographers. When a vacancy opens, they may fill it with an entry-level person at entry-level salary rather than hire an experienced photographer from a smaller station. Commenting on the survey findings, Lee Giles, news director, WISH-TV, Indianapolis, predicts that the seasoned, creative photographer will still find a place. But, he adds, there may be fewer opportunities to move up, and that could hold down salary levels.

CHAPTER 3

Radio Averages

Times have changed since the 1950s, when broadcast journalists were paid about the same in radio and television. By 1992, radio news directors and anchors typically earned only about half as much as their TV counterparts in comparable markets. But for reporters in smaller markets, radio's low pay differed little from television's low pay.

Reporters

The typical radio station has no full-time reporter besides the news director, for whom reporting may be a primary duty. Radio reporters work most often in larger markets. Nearly two-thirds of the ones sampled for the 1991 careers survey were in markets of a quarter-million or more. Only a handful were in small markets, the ones with populations less than 50,000.

With the great majority of reporters located in major markets, it's no surprise that the median of $17,600 and mean of $25,500 in the careers survey were much higher than the $14,500 and $16,320 found when the average station told what it was paying.

TABLE 3.1: Typical Radio Reporters

	Median	Mean	N
All Stations	$14,500	$16,320	92
Major Markets	22,950	23,955	15
Large Markets	16,400	17,340	21
Medium Markets	13,500	14,890	34
Small Markets	12,025	12,340	22
East	17,250	18,875	19
South	12,230	14,850	31
Midwest	14,800	16,660	28
West	13,400	15,410	14

While radio reporters in major markets may be earning only about half as much as TV reporters covering the same story, the $13,500 radio median for medium markets is roughly the same as the $13,845 for TV reporters in comparable TV markets (ADI 151-210). TV stations are seldom found in markets of less than 50,000.

The few radio reporters who work in those smallest markets post the lowest of low pay for broadcast news. At $12,000 a year, their national median is roughly the same as for bartenders and short-order cooks.

Radio reporters earn most in the East and least in the South, where their median of $12,025 is right in there with the $12,045 that Gale Research shows for poultry processors in Georgia.[1]

Anchors/Newscasters

As someone separate from the news director or a rip 'n' read deejay, a newscaster is like a reporter in that not more than half of all stations have such a position. Two-thirds of the radio anchors in the careers sample were in major and large markets. That survey's overall median was $20,070 and the mean was $31,300. Those values appropriately fall between the ones shown in Table 3.2 for major and large markets. The values in the tables, from the 1992 survey of news directors, represent what the average station paid its average anchor.

TABLE 3.2: Typical Radio Newscasters/Anchors

	Median	Mean	N
All Stations	$17,215	$20,325	89
Major Markets	31,400	29,375	22
Large Markets	19,500	19,850	22
Medium Markets	16,985	17,785	29
Small Markets	12,550	13,140	16
East	19,050	23,145	19
South	15,550	17,535	30
Midwest	17,415	20,995	24
West	16,900	21,200	16

The few radio newscasters who have separate positions as such in small markets come about as dirt-cheap as reporters.

In all types of radio news operations, even the few big ones in major markets, most radio newspeople do double duty as reporters and anchors. In the careers survey, they were classified by the duty indicated as primary.

There are well paid radio anchors. Nearly a fourth in the careers survey were making between $50,000 and the top of $120,000, most of them at leading stations in major markets. And be advised that jobs in those newsrooms don't open often. Incumbents tend to stay on. After reading a draft of this chapter, Georgeann Herbert, managing editor at WBBM, Chicago, noted that the station's last opening for a reporter was in 1987. One has been there for 15 years and is "less than halfway up the seniority ladder." Many WBBM anchors and reporters have been with the station for 20 years or more.

Sportscasters

Sports anchors may be the lowest paid members of anchor teams in television, but they average about the same as newscasters in radio. A 1990 survey generated a national median of about $16,000 for each. Across markets, one also makes about as much as the other.

WBBM's Herbert suggests that sportscasters make as much as newscasters in radio, but not television, because sports is more likely to be viewed as a profit center in radio. Play-by-play broadcasts for local teams generate support from advertisers who "tend to be loyal fans who want to show their support for the hometown team."

TABLE 3.3: Typical Radio News and Sports Anchors (1990)

	News		Sports	
	Median	N	Median	N
All Stations	$15,990	118	$15,965	50
Major Markets	27,625	23	28,200	8
Large Markets	16,900	32	16,500	17
Medium Markets	14,960	37	14,930	9
Small Markets	13,180	26	12,050	16
East	17,000	31	21,600	10
South	14,995	29	15,600	15
Midwest	15,035	43	15,060	20
West	20,000	15	16,500	5

Comparisons by markets and regions are not very reliable, because few news directors reported salaries for sportscasters. Whereas sports anchors are part of the news department at most TV stations, they report to news at only two of every five radio stations.

News Directors

The salary that counts most in radio news is the news director's. He or she is the only full-time newsperson at the majority of stations. The median of around $19,000 for 1992 included a gain that beat the cost of living slightly, but for the first time in four years. As we'll see in the trends chapter, radio news salaries have been eroding for many years. News directors now average less than half as much in radio as in television.

TABLE 3.4: Radio News Directors

	Median	Mean	N
All Stations	$19,015	$21,860	217
Major Markets	37,000	39,440	32
Large Markets	23,150	23,495	43
Medium Markets	17,775	18,910	73
Small Markets	15,100	15,810	69
East	21,200	25,545	33
South	18,040	21,180	65
Midwest	17,325	20,430	77
West	21,800	23,425	42

Only news directors in markets of a million-plus exceed the nation's average of $25,400 for everyone with a bachelor's degree only.[2]

Radio news directors do best in the West and East.

Entry Level

Beginners make even less in radio news than in TV news. In my 1991 careers sample of all radio newspeople, the ones who had been out of school a full year or less had a median salary of $12,035, compared to $14,855 for their TV counterparts. Becker and Kosicki surveyed only recent journalism and mass communication graduates who had taken radio news jobs, and they were doing better that year at $13,900 (vs. $14,455 for TV).[3]

The NAB's 1992 radio survey yielded small-market means of $11,615 for reporters and $13,670 for "news announcers." Medium-market averages were $13,035 and $14,550.[4]

As in television, those who had been out of school two years averaged about $2,000 more than beginners. Their median was $14,805 in my 1991 radio careers survey.

Radio and television appear to have adopted an informal trial period between unpaid student internships and regular low-level pay—an initiation of sorts into the "real world." At least that's a possible rationalization for radio and television's paying new graduates so much less than newspapers, PR and advertising.

For years, educators and journalists have lamented the low starting pay.[5] But particularly in broadcast news, the forces of oversupply and profit-centered exploitation join forces to hold entry-level salaries to inappropriately low levels.

Elsewhere at the Radio Station

News directors in radio lack the workplace status of their TV counterparts. NDs are second only to general sales managers among TV department heads. But in radio, they're paid less than just about everyone else who can be called a department head. The 1992 NAB report shows medians of $45,000 for general managers, $45,000 for sales managers, $26,140 for chief engineers, $24,500 for program directors, $24,000 for operations directors and (a big step down this time) $19,000 (same as my survey's median) for news directors. That's from sampling all stations.

By market size, the same story. The news director is the lowest paid. Actually, the chief engineer comes in slightly lower in small markets. But the small-market "chief engineer" is often a part-timer who's on call at an electronics repair shop in case the station's equipment breaks down.

Moving up in the markets means less for news directors than for other key people in radio. NDs increase their pay an average of two and a half times when they go from a small to major market. But sales managers and program directors earn four times as much in major markets. General managers are paid six times as much in the majors as in the minors.

Radio news anchors average about the same as other on-air personalities in all but major markets, where a number of high paid hosts are found.

Even in small and medium markets, stars were paid well in radio's heyday. But those talent dollars long ago moved to television. At the average radio station today, the people who own and run the station make the money. The ones you hear usually don't.

CHAPTER 4

Salary Ranges

The gap between high and low pay in broadcast news is wider than the averages show. Medians tell the story for typical workers, the ones in the middle, but not for the ones at the bottom and top. Sure, there's contrast between the average star anchor's $26,625 in the smallest markets and $263,750 in the largest. Ten times as much. But consider this: The 1992 survey's low for a station's highest paid anchor was $11,000 and the high was $1,000,000. That small-market star had to work 91 days, or three months, to match just one day's pay for the million-dollar anchor in New York or Los Angeles.

Many start at or near the bottom, of course. In 1954, one year out of school and working at a Houston radio station, Dan Rather was making $62.50 a week.[1] (Also a year out of school in 1954, and in radio-TV news in Louisville, I was making $70 a week. But Rather caught up.)

Not bad, actually. Adjusted for inflation, Rather as a beginner was earning $17,000 a year in 1992 buying power. In 1991, entry-level broadcast journalists most often made $13,000 to $15,000.

In 1992, nearly half of the nation's TV stations were paying their average reporters, not just rookies, less than $20,000. One in five paid less than $15,000. Half the radio news directors earned less than $20,000, and a fourth made less than $15,000. At the same time, a fourth of the TV stations had anchors pulling in at least $100,000.

This chapter looks at salary distributions—a study in contrasts.

The tables show graphically how salaries go up with market size. The percentages cluster along a diagonal from bottom pay in ADI 151-210 to top pay in ADI 1-25. No major-market affiliates pay as low as most in small markets. And big-time pay is not found in small markets.

Television

Contrasts, which can serve as an index of the opportunity to move up, are least for basic journalists, most for anchors and above average for newsroom managers.

Basic Journalists

News Photographers

Photojournalists lose in salary ranges as well as averages. Stations in the bottom tier of markets seldom pay as much as $15,000, on average. Not many in ADI 101-150 go over $20,000. Even among ABC, CBS and NBC affiliates in the 25 largest markets, less than half typically pay as much as $40,000. Few stations in ADI 26-50 pay that much.

TABLE 4.1: Typical TV News Photographers

	$9000-14999	$15000-19999	$20000-29999	$30000-39999	$40000-85000
All Markets	24.6%	32.3	25.7	10.4	7.0
Affiliates	26.5%	31.9	26.1	9.2	6.3
Independents	10.0%	35.0	22.5	20.0	12.5
1–25 Affils	.0%	2.5	18.0	33.3	46.2
1–25 Indies	4.0%	24.0	24.0	28.0	20.0
ADI 26–50	.0%	15.7	60.8	21.5	2.0
ADI 51–100	19.6%	39.2	37.5	3.9	.0
ADI 101–150	31.4%	60.5	8.1	.0	.0
ADI 151–210	81.3%	18.7	.0	.0	.0

The typical photographer's base pay as surveyed in 1992 ranged from just over minimum wage in a few of the smallest markets to $85,000 at one ADI 1-25 affiliate.

Reporters

Small-market reporters are poor folks by salary distributions as well as the averages shown in Chapter 3. Nearly two-thirds of stations in the 60 smallest markets pay typical TV field reporters less than $15,000. Advancing to ADI 101-150 takes them only into the upper teens. To find stations that pay in the 20s, reporters must move on up to ADI 51-100.

At the top, most stations at ADI 1-25 affiliates pay typical reporters at least $40,000 and two-thirds pay $50,000. That's still lower than for daily newspaper reporters in those markets. But from the ranks of TV reporters come anchors, whose salaries know no bounds.

TABLE 4.2: Typical TV Reporters

	$9300-14999	$15000-19999	$20000-29999	$30000-39999	$40000-120000
All Markets	18.4%	27.3	28.6	10.7	15.0
Affiliates	20.0%	28.2	28.6	8.8	14.4
Independents	4.9%	19.5	29.3	26.8	19.5
1–25 Affils	.0%	.0	.0	10.3	89.7
1–25 Indies	.0%	8.3	29.2	29.2	33.3
ADI 26–50	.0%	2.0	41.1	35.3	21.6
ADI 51–100	8.5%	29.2	51.0	10.4	.9
ADI 101–150	23.7%	54.8	21.5	.0	.0
ADI 151–210	63.9%	29.5	6.6	.0	.0

Producers

The floor is higher and the ceiling lower for news producers than for reporters. The 1992 survey of stations found one in 10 stations paying average producers less than $15,000, but only one of 12 paying them $40,000 or more. Twice as many stations pay reporters that well. At the top, most ADI 1-25 affiliates pay rank and file reporters at least $40,000, but only half do so for producers.

TABLE 4.3: Typical TV News Producers

	$10500-14999	$15000-19999	$20000-29999	$30000-39999	$40000-84100
All Markets	10.5%	27.2	36.4	17.9	8.0
Affiliates	11.4%	27.9	36.8	16.4	7.5
Independents	3.0%	21.2	33.4	30.3	12.1
1–25 Affils	.0%	.0	.0	47.4	52.6
1–25 Indies	.0%	9.1	40.9	31.8	18.2
ADI 26–50	.0%	6.0	52.0	40.0	2.0
ADI 51–100	5.4%	32.6	55.5	6.5	.0
ADI 101–150	17.8%	49.3	32.9	.0	.0
ADI 151–210	46.9%	37.5	15.6	.0	.0

The station paying typical producers the most listed $84,100, a third less than the highest for reporters. Only three of 231 producers in the careers survey made as much as $100,000. Those with an eye to big money treat station-level producing as a step toward newsroom management.

Assignment Editors

Pay ceilings are also low for the stress champions of TV news, its assignment editors. Most earn less than $50,000. That's even the case at a fourth of the ADI 1-25 network affiliates. Two-thirds of the stations in ADI 150-210 pay assignment editors less than $20,000.

TABLE 4.4: TV Assignment Editors

	$11000-19999	$20000-29999	$30000-39999	$40000-49999	$50000-85000
All Markets	19.7%	34.6	30.0	11.0	4.7
Affiliates	20.8%	34.2	29.4	11.5	4.1
Independents	9.7%	38.7	35.5	6.4	9.7
1-25 Affils	.0%	5.1	35.9	33.4	25.6
1-25 Indies	5.0%	30.0	40.0	10.0	15.0
ADI 26-50	.0%	18.8	60.4	20.8	.0
ADI 51-100	11.4%	46.6	34.0	8.0	.0
ADI 101-150	39.4%	54.5	6.1	.0	.0
ADI 151-210	64.7%	26.5	8.8	.0	.0

Assignment editors are limited by a pay range that sees the largest operations paying about eight times as much as the smallest. That's also the case for producers and photographers. They bump into ceilings sooner than reporters, whose pay is 12 times higher at the top than at the bottom.

Anchors

Typical Anchors

Now we're talking 50 times as much—a range from $10,000 for anchors in the smallest tier of markets to $500,000 for those in the largest. Contrasts abound. One of every eight stations pays typical anchors less than $20,000. One of every eight pays $100,000 or more.

TABLE 4.5: Typical TV Anchors

	$9300-19999	$20000-29999	$30000-49999	$50000-99999	$100000-500000
All Markets	13.6%	21.6	29.8	22.5	12.5
Affiliates	14.5%	21.3	29.7	21.8	12.7
Independents	5.1%	25.7	30.7	28.2	10.3
1–25 Affils	.0%	.0	2.6	15.3	82.1
1–25 Indies	.0%	17.4	26.1	39.1	17.4
ADI 26–50	.0%	2.0	14.3	63.3	20.4
ADI 51–100	5.9%	14.7	51.9	27.5	.0
ADI 101–150	18.0%	39.3	36.0	6.7	.0
ADI 151–210	45.9%	39.3	14.8	.0	.0

Not many stations in the 60 smallest markets pay their average anchors more than $30,000. Few in the 50 largest pay so little—only an indie here and there. The 20s and 30s are modal for ADI 101-150, the 40s for ADI 50-100 and $50,000 to $100,000 for ADI 25-50. A dozen or so of the 75 affiliates in ADI 1-25 pay a quarter-million and up.

That's just for garden variety anchors, average at their stations.

Star Anchors

The highest paid at stations do better. Even the survey's lowest paid star was making $11,000. Multiply that by 91 and up comes $1-million, the 1992 survey's top. For a multiple of 100-plus, put that $1 million against the salary of one of the lean anchors at the station paying an average of $9,300.

TABLE 4.6: Typical TV Station's Highest Paid Anchor

	$11000-24999	$25000-39999	$40000-59999	$60000-99999	$100000-1000000
All Markets	12.2%	22.4	20.9	19.7	24.8
Affiliates	12.7%	22.1	20.0	20.1	25.1
Independents	8.3%	25.0	27.8	16.7	22.2
1–25 Affils	.0%	.0	2.9	2.9	94.2
1–25 Indies	.0%	20.8	29.2	16.7	33.3
ADI 26–50	.0%	5.0	5.0	30.0	60.0
ADI 51–100	5.4%	10.7	31.2	35.5	17.2
ADI 101–150	17.6%	40.0	28.3	14.1	.0
ADI 151–210	39.6%	43.4	11.3	5.7	.0

Practically all ADI 1-25 affiliates pay their top anchor $100,000 or more. Sixty percent go to $250,000 or better. Twenty percent range from half a million to a million. Runner-up to the 1992 station survey's only million-dollar anchor was one struggling along at $900,000.

The 1991 careers survey of staff brought back a questionnaire from an anchor being paid $1.8 million, which may have been the nation's highest at the station level. A newspaper report puts Los Angeles' top at about $1.3 million for Paul Moyer in his six-year, $8-million-plus contract at KNBC.[2]

Some say that's too much, even for network anchors. When CBS News was cutting jobs by the hundreds in the late 1980s, Fred Friendly, its former president, suggested that those making $1 million-plus take voluntary salary reductions to pay the less fortunate. He said, "No journalist requires $1 or $2 or $3 million a year. That's for superstars in show biz—the Redfords, the Streisands, the Newmans—perhaps even for baseball players and football stars."[3]

Others argue that the stars of news are worth as much as the stars of entertainment (the line is blurring) and sports. Don Hewitt, executive producer of CBS's top-rated "Sixty Minutes," responded to Friendly with essentially a—"why not?" Hewitt said,

"We are supported by a multibillion-dollar corporation that sells commercial time to other multibillion-dollar corporations who want to be identified with '60 Minutes' and particularly like the way we draw a crowd to watch their commercials."[4]

Even top-paid network anchors are far behind some of TV's talk show hosts. CBS reportedly lured David Letterman from NBC with $14 million a year.[5] Oprah Winfrey, formerly a TV newswoman in Nashville, is said to have brought in $40 million from her talk show and other enterprises in 1991. The same source lists $1.8 million for ABC anchor Peter Jennings, $2 million dollars for NBC's Tom Brokaw and the usual estimate of $3 million for CBS's Dan Rather.

Chrysler's Lee Iacocca, at $4.5 million, was also far behind Oprah. Mike Tyson made $31.5 million a year at the height of his boxing career. Madonna's material take for 1991 was about $30 million.[6]

Newsroom Managers

Though the talent track leads to the highest salaries, management also carries financial rewards. Second-level newsroom managers, most often executive producers and assistant news directors, are usually paid well in large and major markets. TV news directors draw good salaries in most markets and very good ones in the majors.

Executive Producers

In part because they are seldom found in bargain-basement newsrooms, executive producers fall into pay categories appropriate to professionals in most market categories. Even in the smallest markets, half the newsrooms that have executive producers pay them $20,000 or more. Pay is most often in the 20s and 30s in ADI 101-150 and the 30s in 51-100. In larger markets, it's usually $40,000 and up. A third of the ADI 1-25 affiliates pay executive producers $75,000 and up.

TABLE 4.7: TV Executive Producers

	$11000-19999	$20000-29999	$30000-39999	$40000-49999	$50000-100000
All Markets	11.9%	17.5	29.9	14.4	26.3
Affiliates	12.6%	17.1	30.9	13.7	25.7
Independents	5.4%	21.0	21.0	21.0	31.6
1–25 Affils	.0%	.0	.0	6.1	93.9
1–25 Indies	.0%	18.8	18.8	25.0	37.5
ADI 26–50	.0%	2.6	33.3	35.9	28.2
ADI 51–100	5.9%	21.6	54.9	15.6	2.0
ADI 101–150	34.3%	37.1	28.6	.0	.0
ADI 151–210	50.0%	31.3	18.7	.0	.0

Assistant News Director

Few stations in small and medium markets have assistant news directors. Their salary ranges are similar to the ones for executive producers, though assistant news directors pass them in major markets.

TABLE 4.8: TV Assistant News Directors

	$14000-24999	$25000-39999	$40000-49999	$50000-74999	$75000-110000
All Markets	14.8%	30.5	15.6	25.0	14.1
Affiliates	6.7%	39.1	15.0	25.0	14.2
Independents	.0%	37.5	25.0	25.0	12.5
1–25 Affils	.0%	.0	7.4	40.7	51.9
1–25 Indies	.0%	16.7	33.3	33.3	16.7
ADI 26–50	.0%	.0	19.0	81.0	.0
ADI 51–100	17.6%	47.1	23.5	8.9	2.9
ADI 101–150	34.8%	52.2	13.0	.0	.0
ADI 151–210	46.7%	46.6	6.7	.0	.0

News Directors

The people who run TV newsrooms are paid as managers of profit-centers. Only in a handful of the smallest operations do they earn less than $20,000. A third of all news directors make $60,000 or more. Exact salaries found most often in the survey are stepwise by thousands: $30, $35, $40, $45, $50, $60, $70, $75 and $100-thousand. The steps get longer as you go up.

Even in the smallest markets, nearly two-thirds of all news directors earn $30,000 or more. And they're more likely than their star anchors to make $40,000. ND pay tends to the 30s and 40s in ADI 101-150, the 40s through 60s in 51-100 and from the 60s through 90s in ADI 25-50.

TABLE 4.9: TV News Directors

	$12000-29999	$30000-39999	$40000-59999	$60000-99999	$100000-180000
All Markets	13.0%	21.2	31.6	25.0	9.2
Affiliates	13.6%	20.5	31.5	25.1	9.3
Independents	8.9%	26.7	31.1	24.4	8.9
1-25 Affils	.0%	.0	.0	30.6	69.4
1-25 Indies	7.1%	21.5	25.0	32.1	14.3
ADI 26-50	2.1%	4.2	22.9	64.6	6.2
ADI 51-100	6.1%	15.1	45.5	32.3	1.0
ADI 101-150	16.9%	42.7	38.2	2.2	.0
ADI 151-210	39.3%	27.9	24.6	8.2	.0

Two of every three news directors at ADI 1-25 affiliates earn $100,000 or more. For one in three, it's from $125,000 to $180,000, the 1992 survey's top. That's good pay for managers but still small change for some of the anchors they supervise in those markets.

Radio

Reporters

For a major step down, try the salaries most radio stations pay their reporters. Of the minority of stations employing full-time reporters, a fourth pay them less than $11,000 a year. Half hold it to $14,000 or less. Very few go as high as $30,000.

In small markets, one of every three stations typically pays reporters less than $11,000. Medium and large markets usually average from $11,000 to $20,000. Only a few major-market newsrooms get into the 30s or 40s. But, because those stations employ a substantial share of all radio reporters, a relatively impressive 20 percent of the ones in the careers survey were earning $40,000 or more. The top paid reporter made $100,000.

TABLE 4.10: Typical Radio Reporters

	$8800-10999	$11000-14999	$15000-19999	$20000-29999	$30000-45000
All Markets	19.6%	30.4	31.5	9.8	8.7
Major Mkts	6.7%	6.7	26.6	33.3	26.6
Large Mkts	4.8%	33.3	38.1	19.0	4.8
Medium Mkts	23.5%	32.4	35.3	.0	8.8
Small Mkts	36.4%	40.9	22.7	.0	.0

Anchors

It helps to become a newscaster. Few earn less than $11,000, even in small markets. For all stations surveyed, modal pay for typical newscasters is in the upper teens. One of six pays from $30,000 to $45,000. Only 6 percent went higher. For that reason, no table for "high anchor" is included. The high for the surveys was $120,000, another world from TV anchor highs.

TABLE 4.11: Typical Radio Newscasters/Anchors

	$8800-12499	$12500-14999	$15000-19999	$20000-29999	$30000-55000
All Markets	19.1%	7.9	35.9	20.2	16.9
Major Mkts	4.5%	13.7	18.2	18.2	45.4
Large Mkts	9.1%	9.1	31.8	40.9	9.1
Medium Mkts	10.3%	6.9	55.2	17.3	10.3
Small Mkts	25.0%	43.8	31.2	.0	.0

News Director

As noted in Chapter 3, radio stations sometimes pay news directors more like unskilled laborers than the college-educated professionals most of them are. One of every eight in the 1992 sample was earning no more than $12,000 a year. One of five made less than $13,924, the federal government's poverty level for a family of four in the early 1990s. Radio news directors' salaries ranged from $8,840, the national minimum wage, to $93,000 a year.

As the table shows, the average news director must move to a large market to earn as much as $20,000. In major markets, many remain in the 20s, but about half make $40,000 or more.

TABLE 4.12: Radio News Directors

	$8800-14999	$15000-19999	$20000-29999	$30000-39999	$40000-93000
All Markets	24.9%	27.2	34.1	6.4	7.4
Major Mkts	.0%	9.4	31.2	12.5	46.9
Large Mkts	14.0%	14.0	55.7	14.0	2.3
Medium Mkts	21.9%	34.3	38.3	5.5	.0
Small Mkts	46.4%	36.2	17.4	.0	.0

The highest paid news director in the surveys was making $93,000, compared to the top radio anchor's $120,000. Though the difference is less than in television, major-market radio's ceiling is higher for on-air talent than for news directors. Anchors can be directly related to ratings. In radio, as elsewhere in the mass media and other fields, top money tends to go out to those who get the credit for bringing it in.

CHAPTER 5

Salary Trends

From Churchill Downs to the newsroom, track records are usually the best indicators of future performance. Never a sure bet, of course—we can't predict the future. Even the most astute odds-makers and advanced economic indicators miss quite often. But their projections beat tea leaves or gut feelings, especially over the long term.

How much, for example, will the typical TV news director be earning in the year 2000? We don't know. But my surveys across the years show about $13,000 for 1972, $38,000 for 1987 and $47,000 for 1992. If news directors' pay keeps going up at the average annual rate of the five years from 1987 to 1992, it will approach $66,000 by 2000.

That's only an estimate, a projection of future trends based on past trends and future assumptions. Who knows how times will change from 1992 to 2000? All the projections tell is what to expect if things continue at the rate of recent years.

Trends reported in this chapter point to a growing gap between high paid and low paid broadcast newspeople. Similar trends have been attributed to the larger society by journalists and others in best selling books of the early 1990s. Political analyst

Kevin Phillips writes of a widening gap between the rich and poor in America.[1] Pulitzer Prize-winning reporters Donald L. Barlett and James B. Steele use trends data on U.S. salaries and related variables to document a growing "wealth gap." They conclude that the United States is moving toward a two-class society with ever growing wealth for the haves and downward mobility for the have-nots.[2] What's happening in broadcast newsrooms may well mirror society.

Projections for 2000

Estimates for the year 2000 were generated as follows: The base period chosen for generating projections was 1987-92. The average annual percentage change in median pay was calculated by dividing the dollar change from 1987 to 1992 by five. (Adjustments for compounding were omitted as unneeded for broad estimates such as these.) For positions whose salaries were not ascertained in the 1987 survey, the next nearest year was used. The average annual change percentage was multiplied by eight for estimated 1992-2000 change. Finally, the dollar amount for that percentage increase was added to the 1992 median.

Similarly, projections of the Consumer Price Index for 2000 assume the same average annual increase as for the base period, 1987-92 for most positions. CPI gains have been fairly stable in recent years. At this writing, few economic forecasters were calling for much greater volatility through the 1990s.

Television

Basic Journalists

Photographers, reporters, producers and assignment editors have not kept up with the cost of living in recent years. And, barring priority changes, these basic news handlers can expect their purchasing power to dwindle further in the years to come.

Photographers

Median pay for stations' typical photojournalists increased by a third from 1982 (the first year their salaries were surveyed) to 1992, while the CPI went up half again that much. If we increase the 1982 salary median of $13,520 by the 45.3 percent the CPI inflated, we get $19,650, the 1992 median IF photographers had kept up with the cost of living in that 10-year period. But they didn't.

TABLE 5.1: Trend Medians for TV News Photographers

	All Markets	ADI 1–25 Affils	ADI 151–210	CPI-U
1982	$13,520	$23,660	$10,400	96.5
1987	$15,600 +15.4%	$29,925 +26.5%	$11,960 +15.0%	113.6 +17.7%
1992	$18,120 +16.2%	$38,500 +28.7%	$13,055 +9.2%	140.2 +23.4%
10-Year Change	$4,600 +34.0%	$14,840 +62.7%	$2,655 25.5%	43.7 +45.3%
2000 (at 87–92 avg. ann. rate)	$22,795 25.8%	$56,150 45.8%	$14,960 14.6%	192.7 +37.5%

CPI-U: Consumer Price Index—All Urban Consumers

Market size makes a difference. Photographers bettered the CPI in the 25 largest markets, where union contracts help, and were only a shade under in the ADI 26-50 and 51-100 categories. But they lost to inflation in the bottom 110 markets, enough to throw the national average into earning power's loss column.[3]

> NOTE: This chapter's tables show only the values for total markets, which also serve as middle-market indicators, plus ADI 1-25 affiliates and ADI 151-210, side by side for maximum contrast. Findings for other market categories, including ADI 1-25 indies, are reported in Appendix C.

Photographers did worst in the smallest markets. In those from Odessa-Midland, Texas (ADI 151), to Alpena, Michigan (210), they typically lost $2,000 over 10 years by not keeping up with the cost of living.

Looking ahead, if photographers' salaries keep falling behind and inflation keeps moving ahead at the annual rates for 1987-92, their pay will average just under $23,000 in the year 2000, about $2,000 less than if they kept up with the CPI.

The gap between big-time and small-time will keep getting wider. Photographers at ADI 1-25 affiliates, making three times as much as the ones in 151-210 in 1992, will be making three and a half times as much in major markets as in small markets by 2000.

Reporters

The newspeople who report from the scene have also lost purchasing power in the 10 years their salaries have been surveyed. From 1983 to 1992, stations boosted typical reporters' pay by only three-fourths as much as the cost of living's rise. Had salaries kept pace, the median station would have paid typical reporters $1,800 more than it did in 1992.

Reporters have gained in purchasing power in major markets but lost badly in small ones. At ADI 1-25 affiliates across the nine-year span, their paychecks grew at twice the rate of the CPI. They outpaced it at independents in the 25 top markets and at stations in the next 25. But from there on down, losses to the CPI snowballed—moderate trailing in ADI 51-100, severe lagging in 101-150 and nothing short of disaster in ADI 151-210.

TABLE 5.2: Trend Medians for Typical TV Reporters

	All Markets	ADI 1–25 Affils	ADI 151–210	CPI-U
1983	$15,600	$30,775	$12,530	99.6
1987	$16,900 +8.3%	$33,410 +8.5%	$14,300 +14.1%	113.6 +14.1%
1992	$20,130 +19.1%	$55,500 +66.1%	$13,845 –3.2%	140.2 +23.4%
9-Year Change	$4,530 +29.0%	$24,725 +80.3%	$1,315 +10.5%	40.6 +40.8%
2000 (at 87–92 avg. ann. rate)	$26,285 +30.6%	$114,220 +105.8%	$13,140 –5.1%	192.7 +37.5%

Forget keeping up with the cost of living. Reporters' salaries in the smallest tier of markets have actually been going down. They kept up from 1983 to 1987. Then their profit centers (most of these really small-market stations DO make money on news[4]) cut overhead at the expense of newsroom workhorses. The ADI 151-210 station paid typical reporters $500 less in 1992 than in 1987. At that rate of moving in reverse, they'll be paying reporters $13,100 in 2000 compared to $14,300 in 1987.

Meanwhile at the top, at ADI 1-25 affiliates, 1987-92 was a period of up, up and away for reporters. Their median salary jumped from $33,400 to $55,500, gaining at twice the rate of the CPI. That trajectory would take them to $114,000 by 2000.

The pay gap widens to a canyon when we look at extremes. In 1983 and 1987, ABC, CBS and NBC stations in ADI 1-25 were paying reporters just two-and-a-half times the salaries in 151-210. By 1992, the major league newsrooms were paying four times as much, and the bush league shops were heading the other way. In that scenario, by 2000, reporters will average eight to nine times as much at the top as at the bottom.

Producers

In view of the growing emphasis on production, it's surprising that producers have not kept up with inflation. For all markets combined, the typical station paid producers just $2,000 more in 1992 than in 1984, the first year they made the survey. Their gain for eight years covered only two-thirds of inflation's toll. In the salary disaster area known as ADI 151-210, producers, like reporters, actually were making less in 1992 than eight years earlier. If stations in small markets continue to whittle away as in the 1987-92 base period for our projections, their typical producers will be down to about $14,000 in 2000. Old-timers may then recall the glory year of 1984, when the median was $17,000.

TABLE 5.3: Trend Medians for Typical TV Producers

	All Markets	ADI 1–25 Affils	ADI 151–210	CPI-U
1984	$18,200	$38,495	$16,950	103.9
1987	$18,980 +4.3%	$29,615 −23.1%	$15,600 −8.0%	113.6 +9.3%
1992	$22,145 +16.7%	$39,915 +34.8%	$14,930 −4.3%	140.2 +23.4%
8-Year Change	$3,945 +21.7%	$1,420 +3.7%	−$2,020 −11.9%	36.3 +34.9%
2000 (at 87–92 avg. ann. rate)	$28,055 +26.7%	$62,110 +55.6%	$13,900 −6.9%	192.7 +37.5%

Even at the average annual change rate for 1987-92, smallest-market producers would be making only four to five times less than those at ADI 1-25 affiliates in the year 2000. The gap is less for producers than reporters because their ceiling in the bigtime is lower.

Assignment Editors

Salaries for assignment editors lagged the CPI moderately in most market categories during 1985-92. But overall, they kept up across our criterion 1987-92 period. They should keep pace for 1992-2000.

TABLE 5.4: Trend Medians for TV Assignment Editors

	All Markets	ADI 1–25 Affils	ADI 151–210	CPI-U
1985	$22,100	$35,100	$17,575	107.6
1987	$22,540 +2.0%	$34,475 −1.7%	$18,460 +5.0%	113.6 +5.5%
1992	$28,150 +24.9%	$39,875 +15.7%	$17,875 −3.2%	140.2 +23.4%
7-Year Change	$6,050 +27.4%	$4,775 +13.6%	$300 +1.7%	32.6 +30.3%
2000 (at 87–92 avg. ann. rate)	$39,360 +39.8%	$46,885 +25.1%	$16,965 −5.1%	192.7 +37.5%

Again, the smallest 60 markets stand out as losers. Like reporters and producers, assignment editors in ADI 151-210 lost ground by a few hundred dollars from 1987 to 1992. If that continues, they'll be down to $17,000 by 2000 compared to $18,500 in 1987. It's almost unthinkable that such a downward trend would go on. But the payroll devastation in ADI 151-210 in recent years suggests that nothing is unthinkable in those markets.

Anchors

Typical Anchors

Stations in the 60 smallest markets did somewhat better by their rank and file anchors for 1987-92. Instead of draining the salary pool, they just let it stagnate. In the ADI 51-150 markets, TV stations added some, but raised the pay level only about half as much as the cost of living rose in 1987-92. Average anchors did keep up with the CPI in the ADI 51-100 middle markets, and they outpaced it handily in the 50 largest.

TABLE 5.5: Trend Medians for Typical TV Anchors

	All Markets	ADI 1–25 Affils	ADI 151–210	CPI-U
1983	$23,400	$47,840	$15,600	99.6
1987	$26,000 +11.1%	$84,190 +76.0%	$19,500 +25.0%	113.6 +14.1%
1992	$35,100 +35.0%	$149,585 +77.7%	$19,800 +1.5%	140.2 +23.4%
9-Year Change	$11,700 +50.0%	$101,745 +212.7%	$4,200 +26.9%	40.6 +40.8%
2000 (at 87–92 avg. ann. rate)	$54,755 +56.0%	$335,520 +124.3%	$20,295 +2.5%	192.7 +37.5%

ADI 1-25 anchors are paid like stars. Their median pay went up by three-fourths in 1983-87 and did it again in the five years to 1992. Their pay for the nine-year period grew five times as fast as the consumer price index. No contest—the anchors win.

By contrast, ADI 151-210 stations boosted their pay for average anchors only two-thirds enough to keep up with inflation for 1983-92. In the most recent five years, anchor pay stood still. No contest—inflation wins.

Looking to 2000 by projecting the 1987-92 trend, the average station nationwide will be paying typical anchors upward of $55,000. But, as a median, that number comes from a middle market. In the smallest markets, flat pay for the past projects to flat pay for the future and the 21st century will arrive to find ADI 151-210 anchors averaging a little over $20,000, only $800 more than long ago in 1987.

Most anchors in those small markets wisely have an eye toward larger markets. Projections for ADI 1-25 network affiliates point to typical anchor salaries of a third of a million dollars by 2000—16 times as much as in markets the size of St. Joseph, Missouri, or Eureka, California.

That's a third of a million if you're nothing special. Just second billing. Data for those projections come from asking news directors the salary of their "typical anchorperson." How about their "highest paid anchorperson"?

Star Anchors

Nationwide, stations' highest paid anchors have been beating inflation comfortably and will continue to do so through the '90s if they stay on track—from about $28,000 in 1982 to $50,000 in 1992 to a projected $78,000 in 2000. Those all-markets medians are middle-market.

TABLE 5.6: Trend Medians for Typical TV Station's Highest Paid Anchor

	All Markets	ADI 1–25 Affils	ADI 151–210	CPI-U
1982	$28,080	$85,020	$17,990	96.5
1987	$37,830 +34.7%	$125,890 +48.1%	$24,960 +38.7%	113.6 +17.7%
1992	$50,535 +33.6%	$263,750 +109.5%	$26,625 +6.7%	140.2 +23.4%
10-Year Change	$22,455 +80.0%	$178,730 +210.2%	$8,635 +48.0%	43.7 +45.3%
2000 (at 87–92 avg. ann. rate)	$77,670 +53.7%	$725,840 +175.2%	$29,475 +10.7%	192.7 +37.5%

In ADI 151-210 markets, where TV time sells cheap and newspeople cheaper, even stations' highest paid anchors have been getting low calorie paychecks back to the late 1980s. Through the mid-1980s, they were beating inflation two to one. Then came 1987-92, when the CPI went up as usual, but their pay level barely budged. Rounding to thousands, we see the smallest-market stars go from $18,000 in 1982 to $25,000 in 1987, $27,000 in 1992 and a projected $29,000 in 2000.

While star anchors' pay gains leveled in the smallest markets, they headed skyward in the largest. For ADI 1-25 affiliates, let's talk geometric progression—from $85,000 in 1982 to $126,000 in 1987, $264,000 in 1992 and (hold on to your resume tape) $726,000 projected for 2000.

That's IF the average annual gain rate for 1987-92 continues for the next eight years. Most trends level off. But, for this one, when? Back into the mid-1980s, trade publications have been reporting that stations say they're holding the line on those high anchor salaries.[5] Individual news directors have told me the same thing. But most year's surveys shows star anchor salaries gaining again—and impressively. From 1991 to 1992, they put on another 19 percent. No bets on when they'll level off.

Newsroom Managers

Impresarios, bean-counters and other managers are vital to the profit centers that television newsrooms have become. They're usually paid well in the major leagues, sometimes not so well in the minors.

Executive Producers

These second-level newsroom managers have made only a fair showing in the salary stakes since they went on the survey in 1989. For all markets combined, executive producers have lagged the CPI slightly. They have beaten inflation only in ADI 1-25 and 101-150.

Except in major markets and networks, the salary outlook for executive producers is pedestrian and the ceiling low. But the position is a good steppingstone to higher management.

TABLE 5.7: Trend Medians for TV Executive Producers

	All Markets	ADI 1–25 Affils	ADI 151–210	CPI-U
1989	$31,980	$50,025	$17,890	126.1
1992	$35,105 +9.8%	$64,285 +28.5%	$19,500 +9.0%	140.2 +11.2%
2000 (at 89–92 avg. ann. rate)	$44,265 +26.1%	$113,140 +76.0%	$24,180 +24.0%	182.0 +29.8%

Assistant News Directors

Often promoted from executive producer, the assistant news director normally earns a few thousand dollars a year more. As Tables 5.8 and C.8 show, assistant news directors beat inflation in TV's 50 largest markets from 1988 to 1992, but failed to keep up in ADI 51-150. Though they did well in the smallest markets, that means little because few of those stations have assistant NDs.

TABLE 5.8: Trend Medians for TV Assistant News Directors

	All Markets	ADI 1–25 Affils	ADI 151–210	CPI-U
1988	$34,320	$60,110	$19,000	118.3
1992	$41,000 +19.5%	$81,430 +35.5%	$24,375 +28.3%	140.2 +18.5%
2000 (at 88–92 avg. ann. rate)	$56,960 +38.9%	$139,245 +71.0%	$38,170 +56.6%	192.1 +37.0%

News Directors

Across their 20 years of being surveyed, TV news directors have generally kept slightly ahead of the cost of living. From 1972 to

1992, their salary levels went up almost twice as much as the CPI in the largest operations and lagged it only slightly in small markets. For all markets combined—from about $13,000 in 1972 to $29,000 in 1982, $38,000 in 1987, $47,000 in 1992 and a projected $66,000 in 2000.

TABLE 5.9: Trend Medians for TV News Directors

	All Markets	ADI 1–25 Affils	ADI 151–210	CPI-U
1972	$12,950	$21,190	$10,115	41.8
1977	$18,235 +40.8%	$31,315 +47.8%	$14,040 +38.8%	60.6 +45.0%
1982	$29,380 +61.1%	$52,865 +68.8%	$20,450 +45.5%	96.5 +59.2%
1987	$37,960 +29.2%	$78,155 +47.8%	$28,600 +40.0%	113.6 +17.7%
1992	$47,250 +24.5%	$107,500 +37.5%	$30,880 +8.0%	140.2 +23.4%
20-Year Change	$34,300 +264.9%	$86,310 +407.3%	$20,765 +205.3%	98.4 +235.4%
2000 (at 87–92 avg. ann. rate)	$65,750 +39.2%	$172,105 +60.1%	$33,915 +12.8%	192.7 +37.5%

The gap between news directors' salaries at ADI 1-25 network affiliates at stations in the bottom tier of markets (ADI 151-210) was two to one in 1972. It widened to three-to-one in 1992 and projects to five-to-one for 2000. The medians were roughly $21,000 vs. $10,000 in 1972 and are headed toward $172,000 vs. $34,000 in 2000. As is the case for anchors, top and bottom are becoming different worlds.

Changes in news directors' pay reflect the changing status of local TV news. By the mid-1970s, newsrooms were being touted as profit centers in the 50 largest markets, these larger operations were using consultants, and news directors spent more time coping with ratings and budgets. The better they became as business and talent managers, the more they were paid.

In 1977-82, the profit-center orientation filtered down to middle (ADI 51-100) and medium small (101-150) markets. As newly ordained ministers of bottom lines, their news directors also found they were getting more respect—and money—from the powers that be.

The mid-1980s were lush years for TV news in all market categories. Small-market stations joined the rest in treating newsrooms as profit centers. Accordingly, the price of news directors in ADI 151-210, as in other markets, soared past the cost of living in 1982-87.

Happy paydays continued in 1987-92 for news directors in major and large markets, despite cost-cutting decrees. Managerial expertise became more important than ever at stations where a news ratings point can be worth hundreds of thousands of dollars. So the price of ADI 1-50 news directors outdistanced the CPI during that most recent five-year period. And middle-market news directors kept pace.

But the good times ended for news directors in the bottom 106 markets. To make the kind of profits they wanted from news, stations with low revenue reduced overhead, including pay raises for news directors.

Radio

In the depressed world of radio news salaries, falling behind has long been a way of life. For 20 years, news directors have seen their buying power erode. Newscaster/anchors have done somewhat better.

Reporters

Radio reporters lost purchasing power from 1983, their first year on the survey, to 1987 and again to 1992. They kept pace in the last five years in all but small markets. Trends have been inconsistent, partly because the majority of stations do not have full-time reporters. For that reason, the findings should be interpreted cautiously.

TABLE 5.10: Trend Medians for Radio Reporters

	All Markets	Major Markets	Small Markets	CPI-U
1983	$11,650	$20,850	$10,295	99.6
1987	$13,000 +11.6%	$17,990 −13.7%	$11,650 +13.2%	113.6 +14.1%
1992	$14,500 +11.5%	$22,950 +27.6%	$12,025 +3.2%	140.2 +23.4%
9-Year Change	$2,850 +24.5%	$2,100 +10.1%	$1,730 +16.8%	40.6 +40.8%
2000 (at 87–92 avg. ann. rate)	$17,170 +18.5%	$33,070 +44.1%	$12,650 +5.2%	192.7 +37.5%

Major-market radio reporters outpaced the cost of living from 1977 to 1992, when their median pay was $23,000 and are headed toward $33,000 for 2000. That's higher than the projection for TV reporters in small and middle TV markets, where reporters have been curiously devalued in recent years. At the present rate, by 2000 in medium markets, radio and TV reporters will be earning about the same.

Anchors

Radio newscasters' pay grew faster than the cost of living from 1987 to 1992 after lagging in the previous four-year period surveyed. By 2000, the typical anchor should be earning $24,500. The projected median of $25,310 for radio's medium markets in 2000 is well above the $20,295 projected for TV anchors in the comparable ADI 151-210 markets. Again, such a reversal would result from radio's gaining moderately while television continued to reach new depths of underpaying anchors and other newspeople in those markets.

TABLE 5.11: Trend Medians for Radio Anchors

	All Markets	Major Markets	Small Markets	CPI-U
1983	$13,000	$21,475	$10,400	99.6
1987	$13,625 +4.8%	$23,295 +8.5%	$10,450 +.5%	113.6 +14.1%
1992	$17,215 +26.3%	$31,400 +34.8%	$12,550 +20.1%	140.2 +23.4%
9-Year Change	$4,215 +32.4%	$9,925 +46.2%	$2,150 +20.7%	40.6 +40.8%
2000 (at 87–92 avg. ann. rate)	$24,480 +42.2%	$42,325 +55.7%	$16,585 +32.2%	192.7 +37.5%

In major markets, radio newscasters have outpaced the cost of living. They typically earned $31,000 in 1992 and can expect $42,000 in 2000. That would still be far less than TV anchors in the ADI 26-50 markets, not to mention ADI 1-25.

Small-market radio newscasters almost kept up with the cost of living in 1987-92, but still came up to a median of only about $12,500. At that rate, they'll reach $16,500 by 2000.

News Directors

Overall nationally, radio news directors have been losing to inflation. They were able to buy only a little more than half as much with their pay in 1992 as in 1972. By 2000, it looks like less yet.

Major-market news directors did better than others, but still lost a fourth of their purchasing power over the 20 years. They did edge out the CPI from 1987 to 1992, when their median salary was $37,000. Their 2000 projection—$53,000.

TABLE 5.12: Trend Medians for Radio News Directors

	All Markets	Major Markets	Small Markets	CPI-U
1972	$8,060	$13,260	$7,280	41.8
1977	$10,400 +29.0%	$22,360 +68.9%	$9,100 +25.0%	60.6 +45.0%
1982	$14,300 +37.5%	$29,900 +33.7%	$13,000 +42.9%	96.5 +59.2%
1987	$16,795 +17.4%	$29,120 −2.6%	13,000 .0%	113.6 +17.7%
1992	$19,010 +13.2%	$37,000 +27.1%	$15,100 +16.2%	140.2 +23.4%
20-Year Change	$10,950 +135.9%	$23,740 +179.0%	$7,820 +107.4%	98.4 +235.4%
2000 (at 87–92 avg. ann. rate)	$23,035 +21.1%	$53,020 +43.3%	$19,000 +25.8%	192.7 +37.5%

Small-market radio news directors' paychecks were worth only half as much in 1992 as in 1972. They typically made about $15,000 in 1992 and can expect $19,000 in 2000.

They do it more for love of the job than for money.

CHAPTER 6
Minorities and Women

Salary gaps by race and sex are not always what they seem.

TV news, overall, pays minority staff a little better than whites. But minorities are more likely to be working in major markets. Compute their salary averages separately within market-size groupings, and the minority advantage disappears.

Women in TV and radio news earn less than men. But the women are several years younger and less experienced. Adjust the computations by differences in experience and the male advantage tends to go away.

Most notably, the average anchorwoman earns only two-thirds as much as the average anchorman in TV news. But then, she has been in news only half as long. The big money goes to the many men but few women who have been around long enough to be in their 40s and 50s. Factor in the experience gap and the sex gap closes.

And why are not more women in their 40s anchoring? Dumped for wrinkles? There may be cases of that. But the surveys show a more likely answer. Women became prominent in the TV news work force too late for many of them to have reached their 40s by the early 1990s.

Minorities

Experience as indicated by years in news is about the same for white and minority newspeople in television, typically eight years. And, as Table 6.1 shows, their median salaries are also about the same. Pay was a little higher for minorities than non-Hispanic whites in the 1991 careers survey of more than 1,700 TV journalists. But half of the minority respondents were in the 25 largest markets, where pay is highest, compared to a third of their majority counterparts.

TABLE 6.1: Median Pay by Minority Status

	White	N	Minority	N
Television				
All Positions	$30,000	1465	$31,500	179
Years News	8.1		7.9	
Reporters	$27,050	308	$30,750	62
Photographers	28,450	315	28,750	37
Anchors	37,500	224	46,000	29
In ADI 1–25	34.0%		53.3%	
ADI 1–25 All	$41,000	487	$40,465	91
Reporters	45,835	94	45,500	28
Photographers	35,835	120	39,965	18
Anchors	88,750	46	71,250	11
ADI 26–210 All	$25,160	970	$24,780	85
Reporters	21,300	214	21,750	33
Photographers	20,870	193	21,000	19
Anchors	30,275	177	29,835	18
Radio				
All Positions	$18,915	359	$20,500	24
Years News	7.1		5.2	
In Major Mkts	21.8%		55.6%	
Major Markets	$37,500	81	$34,725	13
Other Markets	17,850	270	13,830	11

How much does market size contribute to the favorability of minority salaries? About the same as for whites. Looking separately at ADI 1-25 and smaller markets, we see a margin for whites that's so small it could be part of normal sampling error.

By position also, minority status makes little difference. Reporters, photographers and anchors—the positions blacks and other minority journalists most often hold—make comparable salaries whether majority or minority. The data indicate little if any salary discrimination by race in television news.

In radio, minorities are also more likely than whites to work in major markets, where the pay is better. Controlling for that variable shifts the advantage substantially to whites both in major markets and those with less than 1-million population. But the survey sample is much smaller for radio, and minorities less often work in radio than TV news. With only 24 minority journalists reporting salaries in radio, the findings should be interpreted with caution.

Results here are consistent with those from a national cross-media survey of journalists by David Weaver and G. Cleveland Wilhoit of Indiana University in 1992. In an article previewing a forthcoming book, they report that no income gap by race was found, except for Native Americans, who make less than others.[1]

Women

There is a sex gap. Women typically earn less than men in broadcast news, as elsewhere in the mass media and in the total U.S. work force, as numerous researchers and writers have pointed out for years.[2]

TV newswomen surveyed in 1991 typically earned 16 percent less than TV newsmen. And as Table 6.2 shows, the male advantage prevails across positions. Newsroom managers, anchors, reporters, producers and assignment editors all make substantially more if they are men. (Photographers are omitted because too few are women for meaningful comparison.)

TABLE 6.2: Median TV News Pay by Sex, Position, Age and Experience

	Male	N	Female	N
All Positions	$31,780	1072	$26,585	579
Years News	9.6		6.2	
Newsroom Mgrs	$45,750	95	$35,000	34
Years News	14.8		10.0	
Anchors	$50,000	119	$31,250	136
Years News	14.2		7.4	
Reporters	$31,665	203	$22,715	169
Years News	9.0		5.8	
Producers	$30,400	88	$25,065	65
Years News	7.3		5.2	
Assignment Eds	$29,250	63	$22,250	32
Years News	9.3		2.7	
Age 20–29	$21,000	168	$19,875	147
30–39	36,500	198	36,875	78
40 & Up	47,500	119	51,500	11
Years News 0–5	$19,340	299	$19,910	249
6–10	30,390	307	32,250	204
11–15	40,000	220	39,700	87
16 & Up	49,800	222	48,500	22

But the men are older and more experienced. Their median age was 32, compared to 26 for the women in TV newsrooms. And that accounts for most of the male-female salary difference. Within age categories, salary averages for men and women differ little—moderately less for women in their 20s, moderately more for women in their 30s and 40s-plus. Those small gaps in pay are nothing like the 16 percent disadvantage shown for women when the gap in age is ignored.

Experience is the variable that really counts. Age per se matters little, but it happens to correlate highly with the years of experience a person brings to a job. Table 6.2 shows that the sex gap in salaries does an even better vanishing act when we control for years worked in news than for age. Median salaries run about the same for men and women who have worked in news the same number of years. The differences of a few hundred dollars one way or the other easily fall within normal sampling error.

The important difference is that only 4 percent of the women in the careers survey had worked in news 16 years or longer, compared to 22 percent of the men. It's their greater experience, not their being male, that gives men higher salaries in the total TV news work force.

In radio, much the same story. Men are older—typically 33, compared to 28 for women. Men have worked in news four to five years longer. And they earn more in the total sample because they overwhelm women with age and experience. Still, women in radio news trail men by only 9 percent.

TABLE 6.3: Median Radio News Pay by Sex, Position, Age and Experience

	Male	N	Female	N
All Positions	$19,845	251	$17,975	135
Years News	9.3		4.8	
Newsroom Mgrs	$19,550	170	$18,400	86
Years News	7.8		5.3	
Anchors	$22,500	37	$17,250	24
Years News	10.1		4.3	
Reporters	$22,875	29	$15,250	22
Years News	9.0		3.3	
Age 20–29	$16,345	83	$16,590	79
30–39	19,960	94	23,300	45
40 & Up	25,310	73	22,500	10
Years News 0–5	$14,450	80	$15,675	72
6–10	19,055	63	20,000	32
11–15	23,750	36	35,500	18
16 & Up	30,500	70	32,750	10

The greatest differences are between men and women as anchors and reporters. As Table 6.3 shows, men typically make far more than women in those radio positions. But, among newsroom managers, including some with such titles as assistant news director, the advantage for men is small.

We shall see later in this chapter (Table 6.5) that the RTNDA-sponsored surveys of news directors in 1991 and 1992 found that women had closed the gap and were earning as much as men.

Let's look further at Table 6.3, from the Freedom Forum-sponsored careers survey of broadcast journalists. With all positions in the mix, the male salary advantage disappears when we control for experience. Indeed, there's an edge or more for women in all categories—five years or less in news, etc.

Here's the male advantage again. Men have been around longer. Twenty-eight percent of the men but only 7 percent of the women have been working in radio news 16 years or more. Thirty percent of the men and 7 percent of the women are 40 or older.

Weaver and Wilhoit conclude from their cross-media survey data that "when experience in journalism is considered, the gender gap in income nearly disappears."[3] Others, including Weaver and Wilhoit,[4] had earlier presented or cited evidence that the gap between women and men has been narrowing both in the mass media and the larger work force.[5]

Male and Female TV News Directors

Now for a sex gap that doesn't wash out.

Television news directors who were women—17 percent of the total in 1992—averaged 31 percent less than male news directors that year. My RTNDA-sponsored survey of news directors showed medians of $49,000 for men and $34,000 for women. That substantial difference challenges the process of looking for an explanation other than sex bias. But, as Table 6.4 shows, numerous efforts were made.

TABLE 6.4: Median Salaries of TV News Directors

	Male	N	Female	N
All NDs	$49,000	338	$34,000	68
Age 21–29	30,050	17	29,400	16
30–39	47,500	122	41,250	28
40–63	54,670	160	60,000	13
Years News 0–5	$28,750	7	$23,000	9
6–10	36,000	43	32,500	18
11–15	45,750	79	43,000	19
16–40	55,375	172	50,375	12
Years Managing 0–2	$30,125	29	$29,500	16
3–5	41,000	64	36,500	18
6–10	50,570	97	50,625	17
11–28	59,970	109	35,750	7
ADI 1–25 Affils	$103,500	28	$115,000	7
1–25 Indies	65,000	19	36,500	9
26–50	73,000	45	60,000	3
51–100	57,875	90	43,750	8
101–150	38,875	67	32,500	21
151–210	33,750	52	25,150	9

Age explains much of the difference. The median age was 34 for female and 40 for male news directors. The youngest women, those in their 20s, were found to make only slightly less than men of that age. The sex gap widens for news directors in their 30s, the age of about half of the women. But it switches in favor of women in the 40-plus age group.

On balance, then, age accounts for much of the difference in pay for male and female TV news directors. It's spurious just to look at the total and say women make a third less. They do, overall—but mainly because the big money goes to news directors who are 40 or older. Fully half of the men, but only a fifth of the women have qualified for 40 candles.

Now, why the reversal at age 40? Why is median pay higher for the few women than for the many men in that maturest of age categories? The survey respondents included a few female managerial stars—women in their 40s who are running some of the nation's largest news operations. And earning $100,000-plus. These women have coped well with the fabled glass ceilings.

Controlling for men's greater experience in the field—a median of 17 years vs. 11 for women—also fails to wipe out the gap between male and female news directors. At every level of experience—from five years down to 16 years up—median pay for the men is moderately higher.

Looking separately at levels of experience in newsroom management gives similar results. Men have typically been managing for nine years vs. four for women. Median pay is roughly the same for male and female rookies, those who had held managerial positions only two years or less, and for those with six to 10 years. Men make substantially more than women who have managed for three to five years and much more than the few women who have managed for 11 years or more.

Controlling for size of news staff also leaves men making more than women, though generally by a small margin, in each category from smallest (0-10 full-timers) to largest (36 and up). The big money, of course, goes to news directors who head the largest staffs, and they're men, six to one.

Again, women got a late start. Very few headed major league newsrooms before the late 1980s. If there's no glass ceiling, the female share of news director positions should grow until it approximates the female share of the work force, which has stood at one-third for several years. At 17 percent, they are halfway there.

Market-size breaks show men earning more than women as news directors at every level—except the top. At network affiliates in the 25 largest markets, median pay is slightly higher for the women. Those few women who have made it into big-time newsroom management are out-earning the male majority.

Male and Female Radio News Directors

In radio, the gap has closed. The 29 percent of news directors who were women in 1992 had a higher median salary than the men. Women outearned men by about 5 percent, or $1,000. Women first caught up in 1991 after gradually narrowing the gap for several years.

Women were ahead by most comparisons. Market-size was the major exception. Median pay for female news directors was higher than for men only in medium and large markets. In the extreme market sizes, small (less than 50,000) and major (1-million and up), male NDs typically earned more than women in 1992. The same market-size pattern was found in 1991. Some of the highest paid radio news directors are men in major markets who have been running newsrooms for decades.

TABLE 6.5: Median Salaries of Radio News Directors

	Male	N	Female	N
All NDs	$18,490	208	$19,500	85
Age 20–29	14,450	40	15,500	34
30–39	19,100	64	22,650	21
40–77	20,970	45	21,750	4
Years News 0–2	$12,650	22	$15,050	14
3–5	15,250	26	17,200	19
6–10	19,625	27	21,750	16
11–55	21,940	74	24,750	15
Years Managing 0–1	$13,750	30	$15,900	19
2–5	17,665	47	19,650	30
6–10	20,170	34	22,500	8
11–40	24,875	34	27,250	5
Major Markets	40,750	17	$28,500	15
Large Markets	23,000	29	24,250	14
Medium Markets	17,500	56	18,250	16
Small Markets	15,950	48	13,350	20

The women in each age category—20s, 30s and 40s-up—averaged more than the male radio news directors. They were also ahead at each level of news experience and years of newsroom management.

Male and Female TV Anchors

The average anchorman earns far more than the average anchorwoman in television. Charges of sex discrimination have brought court cases.[6] There have probably been individual cases of bias against anchorwomen in pay. But my evidence does not support a case for the widespread, insidious bias known as institutional discrimination. Rather, it shows that, on average, male and female anchors with comparable credentials draw comparable pay.

Experience accounts for most of the pay gap. As Table 6.6 shows, the average anchorman has worked in news twice as long as the average anchorwoman. In four out of five categories of years experience in news, median pay was actually a little higher for women than men in the 1990-91 careers survey. Similar results come when male and female salaries are compared separately for anchors in their 20s, 30s and 40s. Anchorwomen in their 20s were averaging about $23,000 and men $22,500. For anchors in their 30s, the medians were $47,500 for women and $40,000 for men. The sample included too few anchorwomen in their 40s for valid comparisons.

TABLE 6.6: Median Pay for Male and Female TV Anchors, by Age and Experience

	Male	N	Female	N
All Anchors	$50,000	119	$31,250	136
Age	38.2	55	29.0	60
Years in News	14.2	125	7.4	144
Age 20–29	$20,250	12	$22,300	31
30–39	41,250	15	47,500	22
40 & Up	98,875	24	112,500	3
0–4 Years News	$17,075	9	$17,550	36
5–7 Years	26,275	18	31,335	35
8–10	35,375	19	43,500	30
11–14	60,500	17	53,250	23
15 & Up	77,500	54	83,750	14

Top pay goes to anchors who are 40 or older, which means having worked in news for at least 15 years. Of all anchors surveyed, 47 percent of the men but only 5 percent of the women were 40 or older. Similarly, 44 percent of the anchormen but only 7 percent of the anchorwomen had worked as long as 15 years in news. With such wide differences, the pay gap comes as no surprise. The salaries of the young women make hardly a ripple when thrown into the pool with those of the older men.

That's also why we so often see a middle-aged anchorman seated with a much younger anchorwoman. She may look to be his daughter. Or, as viewed by pioneer network newswoman Marlene Sanders, anchor teams often look like "second marriages."[7] Actually, the male anchor might prefer someone his own age. But most of the ones available are in their 20s and 30s.

The anchorman's defense for his higher pay is that experience in one's field of work is a valid salary criterion.

Fortysomething Anchorwomen

Why are there so few anchorwomen at local stations who are 40 or older?

Some say it's because her 40th birthday is career doomsday for a TV anchorwoman. Conventional wisdom in some circles is that TV decision-makers don't want wrinkles, sags or spreading dimensions in Barbie, though it's OK for Ken.[8] Such discrimination has been charged.[9] And, given the show biz orientation at some stations, women probably have been dumped from anchoring because they no longer looked like the right stereotypes. But it has not likely happened because of age in many cases.

It could not have happened to great numbers of women in their 40s because too few women that old have ever been in the work force. We easily forget that the advent of women in TV news is recent. In 1972, my first national survey of newsrooms found that the TV news work force was only 11 percent female. That projects to about 950 women, of whom about 250 were anchoring. An estimated 400 others were reporting, but not always seen or heard by viewers. Many TV managers still held to the notion that audiences preferred men on the air, though evidence showed this to be a myth.[10]

To have turned 40 in time for the 1990-91 careers survey, a TV career woman would have needed to be in the work force by the mid-1970s. The number of women in TV news more than doubled from 1972 to 1977, growing to 23 percent, or about 2,400. This surge of female hiring followed a 1971 Federal Communications Commission affirmative action rule that gave women the status a 1969 rule had granted minority groups.[11] Still, only an estimated 600 women (and 2,000 men) were anchoring at local TV stations, and about as many other women were doing on-air reporting.

Normal attrition would have taken half of those women out of television by the 1990s. Women drop out a little more often than men. A 1989 survey found that 3.7 percent of all women and

2.8 percent of all men had left TV news in the previous 12 months. If that dropout rate prevailed across the 14 years for the 2,400 newswomen at TV stations in 1977, no more than 1,200 would have still been in television for the 1990-91 survey. Only half of the women surveyed in the early 70s were as old as 26. So no more than 600 from that pool would have been 40 or older by the early '90s. Among these veterans, let's assume liberally that more than the usual fourth (150) had moved up to anchoring. Even then, it's hard to push the estimate beyond 200-250 of those women who would be in their 40s and anchoring in 1991.

In fact, only about 10 percent of the anchorwomen who were surveyed in 1991, compared to 55 percent of the anchormen, were 40 or older. That's roughly 200 women and 1,600 men from age 40 up. Half of the estimated 2,000 anchorwomen were in their 20s and most others in their 30s. But of 3,000 anchormen, 1,600 were in their 40s and 50s. Their careers began in the 1960s and early '70s before TV news unlocked its doors to women.

So it's no surprise that we find anchormen in their 40s and 50s teamed with anchorwomen in their 20s and 30s. About 750 TV stations were doing news in the early '90s. Even 200 anchorwomen of 40 and up would have been far too few to go around. In fact, these anchorwomen are concentrated at the networks and major-market stations, where they often pull six-digit salaries. Few veteran anchorwomen are found in small markets.

In conclusion, age discrimination has no doubt driven out some women who would now be anchors in their 40s. And it may prove to be a problem for the women who are only now moving into that stage of maturity. But, at this point, normal attrition by the few women in news long enough to be 40 appears the main reason there are no more of them at anchor desks. If the anchorman looks older, he most likely is. And, as seniority would have it, he's probably paid more.

CHAPTER 7
Salary Satisfaction

How well does your pay meet your needs?
 Just fairly well.
 And how does it compare to what you expected when you got into broadcast news?
 It's less.
 Those were the answers that came most often from the 2,100 TV and radio journalists who took part in my 1990-91 careers survey. They were getting by on their paychecks, but not doing as well as they had expected.
 To make more money, do you think you might get out of broadcast news and into some other field?
 Might do it, said just under half of the journalists in television and just over half of the ones in radio. Radio newspeople view their pay less favorably than do their TV counterparts. We have seen that, for the majority of news salaries in television, the cost of living has gone out ahead. For those in radio, it has gone out of sight.
 How important is being happy with one's salary? Other researchers have linked job dissatisfaction with low pay among broadcast journalists in Wisconsin.[1] A study of a major university's

mass communication alumni found a clear relationship between the income and creativity dimensions of job satisfaction.[2] And long before this kind of research began, Adam Smith wrote, "The wages of labour are the encouragement of industry, which, like every other human quality, improves in proportion to the encouragement it receives."[3]

Meeting Needs

Television

Careers survey respondents were asked to "rate" their salaries by answering the question: "How well is your present job meeting your salary needs?" Choices: "very," "fairly" and "not" well.

TV journalists of the 1990s are less than elated by their pay. Not more than one in five survey respondents had salaries that met their needs "very" well. One in four said their pay did not meet their needs. The majority said "fairly" well.

Women were somewhat less likely than men to see their salaries as adequate. This may come from their being younger. As shown in Table 7.1, salary satisfaction ratings go up with age. So do salaries.

White and minority respondents had similar perceptions of how well pay was meeting their needs.

The rookie effect shows clearly in the age breaks. Two of every five TV journalists in their 20s said salaries were not meeting their needs at all well. Those in their 30s and 40s most often said fairly well. A third of the ones in their 40s said they were doing very well.

The larger the TV market, the higher the salary satisfaction. And salary. No surprise, since newspeople in larger markets are older and more experienced, and the stations bring in more money. But there's still another factor. Stations in small markets are exploiting the oversupply of eager young college graduates by paying rock bottom salaries. More than half the ADI 151-210 respondents said their pay was inadequate. So did a third of the ones in ADI 51-150 markets. The surest way to make ends meet is to get a job at a station in one of the 50 largest markets.

TABLE 7.1: How Well TV News Pay Meets Needs

	Very Well	Fairly Well	Not Well	N
All Staff	18.8%	53.7	27.5	1,702
Male	21.2%	55.8	23.1	1,096
Female	14.7%	49.8	35.4	604
White	19.4%	53.6	27.0	1,502
Minority	14.7%	53.4	31.9	191
Age in 20s	13.1%	45.3	41.6	329
Age in 30s	20.3%	57.7	22.0	291
Age 40 & Up	35.7%	51.6	12.7	126
ADI 1–25	24.2%	57.0	18.8	607
ADI 26–50	25.7%	57.0	17.3	307
ADI 51–100	13.3%	51.5	35.2	421
ADI 101–150	10.5%	52.9	36.6	238
ADI 151-210	9.4%	35.9	54.7	117
Newsroom Mgrs.	32.1%	51.1	16.8	137
News Anchors	26.4%	49.2	24.4	258
Weathercasters	25.6%	57.7	16.7	78
Photographers	18.3%	56.3	25.4	252
Producers	15.7%	50.8	33.5	236
Sportscasters	13.9%	59.3	26.9	108
Assignment Eds.	13.0%	53.0	34.0	100
Reporters	12.6%	54.6	32.8	390

Need-meeting differs by position, as do salary levels. Newsroom managers were the most likely to say their pay was meeting their needs very well. Reporters were the least likely. As for anchors, about as many said they were not making it at all as were making it very well—half said fairly well. Keep in mind that some small-market stations pay anchors more in celebrity status than in money. (This means they'll recognize you in the supermarket —as you hand the checkout clerk the food stamps.) Elsewhere around the anchor desk, weathercasters get by better than sportscasters.

86 | Let's Talk Pay in Television and Radio News

Producers and assignment editors are down there with reporters as hardship cases. Interestingly, they are more likely than photographers, the lowest paid news staff (but stoics?), to say it hurts.

Consider extremes—the roughly 5 percent of TV newspeople earning less than $14,000 and the 5 percent earning $100,000 or more. It's no surprise that 71 percent of the lowest paid said their income was meeting their needs "not at all" well. But if you think practically all of the highest paid checked "very" well, you're wrong. Only 58 percent did. Some always strive for more, and that probably helped them get to $100,000 in the first place.

TABLE 7.2: How Well Radio News Pay Meets Needs

	Very Well	Fairly Well	Not Well	N
All Staff	12.4%	51.1	36.5	395
Male	14.3%	54.3	31.4	258
Female	8.8%	45.2	46.0	137
White	12.3%	50.7	37.0	365
Minority	14.8%	51.9	33.3	27
Age in 20s	3.6%	47.0	49.4	166
Age in 30s	14.0%	55.9	30.1	143
Age 40 & Up	26.5%	51.8	21.7	83
Major Markets	30.5%	46.3	23.2	95
Large Markets	3.8%	53.2	43.0	78
Medium Markets	8.8%	56.9	34.3	137
Small Markets	6.6%	44.7	48.7	76
Anchors	20.0%	48.3	31.7	60
Reporters	12.5%	46.4	41.1	56
News Directors	10.9%	50.4	38.7	230

Radio

"Seek and you shall find" often does not apply in radio news. Only one of every eight radio journalists said their salaries were meeting their needs very well. And that response came mainly in major markets. In markets of under a million population, a third to a half said their needs were not being well met. Those in small markets fared worst.

Minority status made no difference. And the women of radio news felt dollar crunches more often than did the men.

Younger workers average lower salaries. In radio as in television, staff in their 20s felt financial binds more often than those in their 30s, who, in turn, saw needs unmet more often than the ones 40 or older.

Meeting Expectations

Television

Nearly half of the people working in TV news are disappointed with their pay.

Question: "How's your salary compared to what you expected by now when you entered the field? More? Less? Or about the same?"

"Less" was checked by nearly half of the survey respondents. And about the same number said pay might cause them to get out of broadcast news.

Women were slightly more likely than men to say salaries did not meet their expectations, but no more likely to say that pay might make them quit the field.

Minority journalists were disappointed in salaries more often than whites, but were less likely to say this might drive them from TV news.

The younger the news staff, the more of them said salaries were not up to expectations and could send them to other occupations. More than half of all staff in their 20s said they had seriously considered leaving broadcast news for higher income.

TABLE 7.3: How TV News Staff View Their Pay

	Salary Compared to Expectations When Entered the Field			May Drive from Field	N
	Less	Same	More		
All Staff	47.7%	32.0	20.3	44.4%	1,730
Male	44.4%	33.2	22.4	45.8%	1,112
Female	53.5%	30.0	16.5	42.1%	617
White	46.5%	32.9	20.6	45.7%	1,526
Minority	57.1%	24.5	18.4	36.1%	196
Age in 20s	53.7%	32.8	13.4	56.3%	335
Age in 30s	45.4%	33.6	21.0	43.4%	295
Age 40 & Up	39.7%	27.5	32.8	28.1%	131
ADI 1–25	41.5%	32.0	26.5	32.3%	615
ADI 26–50	41.8%	31.3	26.9	33.6%	316
ADI 51–100	54.4%	32.3	13.3	57.8%	430
ADI 101–150	52.5%	33.1	14.4	58.2%	236
ADI 151-210	62.5%	30.1	7.5	59.7%	170
Newsroom Mgrs.	37.1%	31.8	31.1	33.3%	132
Weathercasters	37.5%	31.3	31.3	30.0%	80
Sportscasters	40.2%	34.8	25.0	42.1%	112
News Anchors	47.4%	27.8	24.8	35.6%	270
Assignment Eds	47.5%	29.3	23.2	47.1%	99
Photographers	47.5%	34.4	18.1	51.0%	259
Reporters	51.9%	35.9	12.2	49.0%	391
Producers	56.0%	26.6	17.4	49.8%	241

Only in the 50 largest markets, did the majority of TV news staff say their salary expectations were being met or bettered. In those markets, one in four was exceeding expectations, and only one in three had considered leaving the field because of pay. But in middle and small markets, the majority said pay was not what they had expected and might drive them from broadcast news.

Let's look at salary satisfaction by positions. Half of the producers, reporters, photographers and assignment editors who, in combination, make up two-thirds of the work force, said their salaries were not meeting expectations. Also, about half said low pay might drive them from TV news.

News anchors, though better paid than other staff, were

about as likely as others to sing the salary blues, but not as likely to be looking for a better paying occupation.

Weather and sports anchors thought they were doing pretty well. (The overall contentment of weathercasters may even be related to the finding, in a study to be published later, that they are less likely than any other staff to have job-related health problems.)

Of all TV news personnel, only news directors were as pleased with their pay as were the weathercasters. Roughly a third of the news directors were making more, a third less and a third about the same as they had expected when they got into broadcast news.

TV journalists with salaries of $100,000-plus were being paid beyond their early dreams in two thirds of the cases. A fifth were making about what they had expected. For one in eight, pay was not up to expectations.

Of those making less than $14,000, three-fourths said they had hoped for more. All others were meeting expectations, except one who felt overpaid.

Radio

Disappointment was the rule in radio news, where nearly two thirds of the careers survey respondents said their salaries were not up to expectations. More than half said they had seriously considered leaving broadcast news for better pay.

Women and minorities were slightly less contented than white men.

Age made less difference than in television. Radio newspeople in their 30s had about the same frustration level as those in their 20s. Even half of the ones who were 40 or older were earning less than expected.

Only respondents in radio's major markets had earnings as high as they had hoped for—and a fourth in those markets had exceeded expectations. In small markets, on the other hand, three-fourths were frustrated with pay, and only three of 81 respondents were making more than expected.

Radio news directors were more likely than anchors or reporters to say their salaries had let them down and they might be looking to the greener pastures of another occupation.

TABLE 7.4: How Radio News Staff View Their Pay

	Salary Compared to Expectations When Entered the Field			May Drive from Field	N
	Less	Same	More		
All Staff	63.8%	23.5	12.7	55.9%	395
Male	61.8%	24.4	13.8	60.4%	254
Female	67.4%	22.0	10.6	58.9%	141
White	63.0%	24.2	12.8	60.7%	368
Minority	76.0%	16.0	8.0	48.0%	25
Age in 20s	67.1%	24.7	8.2	67.2%	170
Age in 30s	66.9%	20.9	12.2	61.9%	139
Age 40 & Up	52.4%	24.4	23.2	43.8%	82
Major Markets	47.9%	23.4	28.7	40.4%	94
Large Markets	74.4%	16.7	9.0	70.7%	78
Medium Markets	62.2%	28.1	9.6	64.1%	135
Small Markets	74.1%	22.2	3.7	66.3%	81
Anchors	55.9%	27.1	16.9	50.8%	59
Reporters	60.0%	25.2	14.5	57.6%	55
News Directors	67.9%	20.9	11.1	64.3%	234

CHAPTER 8

Overtime

For a few youthful years at WHAS-TV, Louisville, I lived on overtime. Base salary was for subsistence—food, housing, automobile and other necessities. Overtime was for living—jazz festivals, travel and the other good things of life in the 1950s and early '60s. Even with a second-string managerial title, I was paid time and a half for all hours over 40 and double time for holidays.

Overtime pay was also a way of life in the few months of my first job at 250-watt WKAY AM, county seat radio in Glasgow, Kentucky. Working extra to deejay "The Sunshine Gospel Hour," for example, paid time and a half. That was in dollars, not compensatory time.

Paid overtime is no longer so easily available. From small-market radio to large-market television, my surveys show, newspeople work more than 40 hours a week—typically 46 in radio and 48 in TV. But they are often not paid for those extra hours.

If you're salaried and ineligible for overtime, expect to work longer hours. That's the rule in broadcasting, as in the nation's larger work force.[1] Most of TV's newsroom managers are exempt from paid overtime, and they put in an average of 55 hours a week. Most photographers are non-exempt hourly wage earners, and they average 45. In between—some exempt and others not—reporters, producers and assignment editors typically work 48 to 50 hours a week. Anchors most often are under salary contracts and don't get overtime pay. But at 49 hours a week, the typical anchor still works the equivalent of a six-hour day less than her or his supervisor.

Who must be paid for overtime under the Fair Labor Standards Act of 1938? At this writing, rulings have been less than definitive. In general, the law mainly exempts "learned professionals," "artistic professionals" who do "work that is original and creative in nature," and people whose work requires advanced knowledge "acquired by a prolonged course of specialized instruction," as well as executives and administrators. General assignment reporters, producers, directors and assignment editors at KDFW-TV, Dallas-Fort Worth, do not meet exemption criteria and must be paid overtime, according to a federal court ruling in 1990. The court said that what matters is the job description rather than the title. The ruling tends to be case-specific, leaving clearer guidelines for perhaps a later lawsuit.[2]

Television

A 1991 RTNDA-sponsored survey asked news directors which of their staff were eligible for overtime.

Most TV stations classify at least some news staff as eligible. Only 8 percent of the NDs responding to that part of the survey said no one was. Not one network affiliate in the 50 largest markets said no one qualified for paid overtime. But at one of every five newsrooms in the 60 smallest markets, no-overtime was the rule.

Photographers qualify for overtime at most stations. Even in newsrooms where no one else may do so, ENG photographers put in for overtime. As Table 8.1 shows, they're eligible at eight to nine of every 10 stations in most market categories. Practically all ADI 1-25 network affiliates pay photographers overtime. So do nearly two-thirds of the ADI 151-210 stations. In most markets, photographers get their time and a half.

TABLE 8.1: % of TV Newsrooms with Staff Eligible for Overtime

	No One	Photogs.	Reporters	Producers	Asgnmt. Eds.	Anchors	N
All stations	8.4	84.3	67.2	37.4	15.7	14.9	369
1–25 Affils	.0	97.1	42.9	42.9	25.7	14.3	35
1–25 Indies	13.0	82.6	30.4	30.4	4.3	8.7	23
ADI 26–50	.0	87.2	68.1	40.4	23.4	17.0	47
ADI 51–100	8.4	89.1	79.0	39.5	13.4	13.4	119
ADI 101-150	6.7	80.1	75.3	30.3	12.4	13.5	89
ADI 151-210	21.4	62.5	50.0	30.4	16.1	23.2	56

Reporters are the iffy ones. Overall, two-thirds of the responding stations pay reporters for overtime. Market size is related curvilinearly. The largest and smallest markets are least likely to let reporters collect overtime, and those in the middle most likely. Less than half of ADI 1-25 network affiliates do; instead, they put reporters on fixed-salary contracts as talent along with anchors. Upward of three-fourths of the stations in large and middle market stations pay reporters overtime. Only half do in ADI 151-210. In quite a few small-market newsrooms, 50-60 hours a week at base pay is the rule. Take it or leave it, they say, fresh college grads are waiting in line to work unlimited hours at $13,000 a year.

In keeping with the apparent guideline that duties and credentials rather than job titles make the difference, one of every eight stations in 1991 was paying overtime to some reporters but not others. For example, a station may pay overtime to general assignment reporters but not to a veteran reporter who specializes in government and politics.

Producers are considered exempt twice as often as reporters. Only a third of the stations were paying overtime to producers. Seven percent said yes for some and no for other producers. More often than not, in large markets and small, producers are treated as creative or decision-making professionals for whom fixed salaries are appropriate.

Assignment editors are exempt from overtime pay at most stations. But a federal court said KDFW-TV must pay them overtime. It may depend on interpretations of "managerial." Assignment editors typically administer news budgets, not dollar budgets. They dispatch staff to news stories, but don't grant them raises or promotions. And, as is the case for reporters and producers, their duties and authority vary from one station to the next, or even within the same newsroom.

Anchors at most TV stations are not paid extra for the nine hours they typically work beyond 40. For one thing, paying time and a half for those nine hours to, say, a $400,000 anchor would bring her pay up to about $450,000. That's not about to happen, of course, in small markets, where anchors are the most likely to get overtime. Also, in markets of all sizes, they tend to be on talent contracts to do a job for whatever hours it takes.

Executive producers (not included in the table) are generally considered second-level newsroom managers. They are eligible for overtime at only about one of 10 stations, most often in smaller markets.

News directors, assistant NDs and managing editors are nearly always considered managerial and ineligible for overtime.

Radio

Don't count on using overtime to supplement low base pay in radio news. Three-fourths of the stations in the survey were paying no newsperson overtime. For reporters and anchors, overtime was least likely at stations in small and medium markets, where pay is the lowest. Only one of every five newsrooms in those smaller markets pay overtime, compared to two of five in major markets.

TABLE 8.2: % of Radio Newsrooms with Staff Eligible for Overtime

	No One	Reporters	Anchors	News Dir	N
All stations	77.0	13.9	9.1	11.5	188
Major Mkts	60.7	28.6	32.1	7.1	28
Large Mkts	74.5	19.6	13.7	13.7	51
Medium Mkts	80.0	10.6	5.9	11.8	85
Small Mkts	80.2	9.3	2.3	11.6	86

Policies on overtime for radio reporters and anchors may differ less by market size than the table indicates. The question asked whether they were eligible, and percentages come from dividing "yes" checks by all stations giving salary information. That approximates the share of stations paying overtime. But, particularly in small and medium markets, many stations do not have reporters or anchors as part of the news staff.

Of the stations telling pay for full-time reporters, 44 percent said they were eligible for overtime. The shares ranged from two-thirds in major markets to one-third in small markets.

News anchors could collect overtime at 69 percent of the major-market and 25 percent of the small-market stations surveyed. Those numbers go along with the table's showing that radio news staff are twice as likely to earn overtime pay in a major market as in a small market.

Radio news directors are eligible for overtime at only one of every 10 radio stations. Market size makes little difference. But staff size does. NDs can collect for overtime at 20 percent of the stations where they are the only full-time newsperson, but at only 8 percent of the ones where they have someone to supervise.

As Part of the Salary Budget

"Of total pay to the news staff, how much is overtime?"

That question has not been on a survey in recent years. But when it was asked in 1981, most TV and radio newsrooms that paid overtime were holding it to 10 percent or less. Three fourths did so. And about as many said 6-10 percent of the salary budget went to overtime as said 1-5 percent. Only one of every four stations offering overtime let it exceed 10 percent of the total payroll.

Small-market TV stations that paid overtime were less likely than those in major markets to go over 10 percent. But in radio, market size made no difference on that count.

Overtime can take a sizable chunk of a newsroom's salary budget. As cutbacks became epidemic in the early 1990s, my surveys found that, for big savings fast, stations most often reduced staff. But for cutting costs in day to day operations, they most often cracked down on overtime.

One of every four TV stations had cut back on overtime between mid-1991 and mid-1992. That was about the same across market-size categories.

Nine percent of the radio sample had trimmed overtime. But that finding needs qualifying. Only 23 percent had any overtime to cut because they were not paying it to start with. This means that overtime became harder to get in one out of three of the radio newsrooms that paid it.

Overtime cutbacks also took place in the 12 months preceding the 1991 survey, though not as widely as in 1992. And new ones were expected to show up in the 1993 survey. Overtime is a vulnerable budget item.

But shifts and stories still get covered by staff who are eligible for overtime. As noted on numerous questionnaires, stations are increasingly substituting compensatory time. You work the extra hours now and get compensated later with some time off. And suppose you need money more than time off? Too bad, they say, times are hard.

Overwork

Or maybe you'd like more quality time away from work—without sacrificing pay. A 40-hour work week was the intent when President Franklin D. Roosevelt signed the Fair Labor Standards Act in 1938. And for two or three decades, we were headed in that direction. Then the trend reversed and people started working longer hours. In broadcast news, they now typically put in 45 to 55 hours a week, depending on the position.

In some cases, employees are required to work paid overtime when they'd rather have the time than the money. Veteran labor reporter Dick Meister:

> *That's mainly because it's generally cheaper for employers to pay current employees the overtime rate than to hire new workers to do the work at the regular rate. They must provide fringe benefits to them as to all employees and meet other heavy costs involved in hiring people these days.*[3]

As we have seen, the people who work the longest hours in broadcast news are not the hourly workers, but the newsroom managers who are exempt from overtime pay. Their 55 hours weekly is only a median. Looking at extremes, we find a mere 3 percent who say they work no more than 40 hours and 14 percent less than 50. Thirty percent work 60 or more. Four percent put in 70 to 80 hours a week.

Workaholics are in the mix, and you may be pressured to act like one. Even if you are good enough to do the job in 40 hours, a Kafkan workplace may expect you to spend 55 at it, as others do. Harvard economist Juliet B. Schor writes that workaholism is:

> *...to some extent a creation of the system...As long as there are even a few workaholics, competition will force others to keep up. Employers*

> *will prefer the hard workers... This suggests that the workaholic can set the standard to which others are compelled to adhere.*[4]

Schor argues that overwork is in part a product of unrelenting profit orientation in times of economic stress.

> *The 1980s were a period of increased overtime and reductions in vacations, rest periods and other paid time off. Among better-paid white-collar employees, large-scale layoffs and the cutthroat environment made greater commitment of time and energy necessary to retain one's job. At the low-wage end of the labor market, sweatshops reappeared, with nineteenth-century style conditions. The government contributed by eroding legal protections for employees, as well as failing to enforce existing regulations.*[5]

Like wage and hour laws?

In addition, government figures cited by Schor show that hourly workers have lost buying power in the past two decades.[6] Similarly, my surveys show that the biggest losses to inflation have been taken by the broadcast journalists who are most often paid on an hourly basis, most notably photographers and reporters. They now work more hours but can buy less.

CHAPTER 9

Interns

The lowest pay is no pay. That's what hundreds of interns take home for working 10 to 40 hours a week in television and radio newsrooms.

In lieu of money, most are "paid" in college credits. They get real-life experience that's unavailable on their campuses. And they gain an edge in the extreme competition for regular paying jobs.

Stations often gain by increasing news staff without adding payroll or benefit costs. But, at least for internships worthy of the name, regular staff invest many hours of supervisory time to provide these fledgling journalists an enriching educational experience.

Sounds like something every student would want? Most do. And that brings us to a downside. Students by the thousands now seek internships, and stations say they can meet the demand only by offering them without pay. If stations follow federal regulations, unpaid interns get diluted experience—they are severely restricted in the work they are allowed to do. Paid internships are worth more professionally as well as financially, but are available to few of the many students who may want them.

The Unpaid Take Over

Time was when many journalism schools recognized only paid internships, and the majority of TV and radio stations that offered internships paid students for their work. At the University of Wisconsin-Madison in the early 1970s, we granted journalism credit for internships only through a seminar taken later. A paid internship was a prerequisite for the seminar. We reasoned that anyone can work free. The few students we were ready to recommend for internships had too much to offer to give their work away. They had taken rigorous courses in news writing, basic reporting and camera-reporting. With minimal breaking-in, they were ready to do work that justified pay. They did so and newsrooms were happy with them, year after year.

But then, word spread that television news was the most glamorous career this side of Hollywood. Communication enrollments burgeoned. Young men and women knocked on newsroom doors, willing to work free to get a start. Stations came under pressure from universities to provide internships to most students who wanted them. Stations couldn't put them all on payrolls. So unpaid internships came into their own, and found takers. Selectivity became a casualty. Elitism became a dirty word. And by the early 1980s, the Wisconsin seminar had no choice but to recognize unpaid internships.

To see what happened, let's compare RTNDA-sponsored surveys conducted 15 years apart. Unpaid internships, once rolling, tended to crowd the paid ones off the road. In 1976, 57 percent of the TV and 81 percent of the radio stations with interns paid at least some of them. By 1991, only 21 percent of the TV and 32 percent of the radio stations with interns were paying.

Counting interns instead of stations, 45 percent of the ones in TV news were paid in 1976—10 percent in 1991. In radio, 80 percent of all interns were paid in 1976, 21 percent in 1991.

In both years, radio was less likely than television to have news interns of any kind. But, as Table 9.1 shows, when radio stations did have interns, they were more likely than the ones in TV to be paid.

TABLE 9.1: Newsrooms' Changing Use of Interns

	Television		Radio	
	Paid	Unpaid	Paid	Unpaid
Using Interns				
1976	27.4%	25.4%	18.6%	4.4%
1991	17.7%	76.5%	8.2%	17.6%
Average per Term in Newsrooms with Interns				
*1976	1.5	2.0	1.2	1.3
1991	1.9	4.0	1.4	1.7
Estimated Summer Number				
1976	260	315	1,200	310
1991	260	2,320	670	1,735
Estimated Total Interns				
1976	520	630	2,400	620
1991	520	4,640	1,340	3,470
Est. Full-Time Work Force				
1976	9,000		12,000	
1991	20,400		10,500	
Estimated Ex-Interns at Same Station Hired 1991	800		1,015	
Share of All Hires	17.4%		18.8%	

*Not ascertained in survey, but adapted from other year's values.

Academic credit was awarded for internships served at 84 percent of the TV and 66 percent of the radio stations in 1976. The 1991 survey didn't ask that, but one would expect an even higher percentage. The growing use of unpaid interns goes with compensating in college credits instead of money.

Growing Numbers

Many more radio and TV stations offer internships today than in the mid-1970s. The number of TV newsrooms using summer interns went up from 48 percent in 1976 to 85 percent in 1991.

Radio stayed at 25 percent. Many new stations went on the air during the 15 years, too. News operations increased from about 625 to 750 in television, and from 5,400 and 5,800 in commercial radio.

Paid internships are still out there. Indeed, TV news had as many in 1991 as in 1976. Surprised? I was when I multiplied the averages by the stations with interns and came up with the same projected 260 paid interns for each year. (This comes from more stations in 1991, and more interns per station.) Radio, on the other hand, cut its paid interns by almost half.

But it's unpaid interns who exploded the totals. Seven times as many were in TV newsrooms in 1991 as in 1976. Radio's increase was fivefold.

The 1991 survey asked about only summer interns. But Table 9.1 gives estimates for total interns. Here's how. The 1976 survey found that roughly as many stations used interns during the regular academic year as in summer. Educators and industry leaders indicate that's still the case. We also know that turnover takes place each term, but that many students serve more than one term. The rough estimates of 12-month totals for 1991 come from letting repeaters cancel out term turnover, and thus multiplying summer values by two terms instead of three. (If you prefer another multiple, plug it in and see what you get.)

Now, think for a moment about those totals—roughly 5,000 students interning in TV newsrooms and 5,000 in radio every year. Compared to 1,100 in TV and 3,000 in radio back in the mid-1970s. In the summer months and probably during the academic year, that's one intern for every eight regular full-time news employees in television and one for every four in radio. Interns everywhere you turn. Newsrooms have had to add work stations. And while they have not often let interns increase payrolls, stations have absorbed costs in the form of supervisory time and overhead (facilities don't come free).

TV newsrooms with unpaid interns typically have three or four. But a third have five or more. In the 25 largest markets, two-thirds have five or more and nearly a fourth have 10 or more—up to 25 unpaid interns at a time. You need a classroom just to sit them down together. Some newsrooms even have assistant or associate news directors primarily to supervise interns. They're *de facto* faculty for universities.

Again, that grand total—roughly 10,000 students a year are working as interns and hoping to get regular jobs in broadcast journalism. Such a number suggests that supply exceeds demand. It does. Special surveys I did in the mid-1970s showed that broadcast news job applicants outnumbered entry-level jobs by at least two to one. If only broadcast news majors applied, there might be too few for the openings. But add applicants from other communication areas and outside majors like history and political science, and there's a major oversupply.[1] Add the media economic crunch of the early 1990s, and the applicant lines grow still longer.[2]

Pipelines to Payrolls

That's when internships pay off—at hiring time. Interns are favored applicants in the growing competition for jobs. In both television and radio, former interns at the station account for at least one of every six hires. As Table 9.1 shows, the typical TV newsroom had hired one of its former interns in the 12 months before the 1991 survey. For every three interns on the job during the year, one ex-intern was going on the regular payroll. In radio, former interns were well over half of all hires.

If it doesn't happen by graduation day, maybe later. You may have excelled as an intern, but there's no opening. Or, especially if you interned at a major-market station, you may need to get experience in a smaller market first. But do a good job as an intern and they'll remember. That's clear from the finding that the ex-interns who were hired equaled 96 percent of all entry-level hires. It's implausible that practically all entry-level hiring would be of ex-interns. What that high percentage says is that former interns are also prominent among the staff hired from other stations. Either way, when the number of ex-interns hired by a station roughly equals all of its entry-level hires, we're talking an advantage in the job market.

Former interns hired by radio newsrooms numbered 57 percent as many as all people hired just out of college.

Further endorsement of internships as pipelines to payrolls come from the 1990-91 Freedom Forum-sponsored survey of journalists. As Table 9.2 shows, half of the broadcast newspeople working today—three in five for TV and two in five for radio news—are former interns. And time after time in the careers survey, they said interning was one of their most valuable college experiences.

TABLE 9.2: Journalists' Use of Internships

	Unpaid Only	Paid Only	Paid & Unpaid	None	N
All TV	37.6%	10.8	8.8	43.1	1,781
Men	32.2%	10.2	7.5	50.1	1,142
Women	47.2%	11.7	11.2	29.9	632
Whites	38.1%	11.0	8.0	42.9	1,565
Minorities	33.2%	8.9	15.3	42.6	202
All Radio	27.1%	10.1	4.8	58.0	414
Men	22.8%	9.7	3.3	64.2	268
Women	34.9%	11.0	7.5	46.6	146
Whites	26.6%	9.4	4.9	59.1	384
Minorities	33.3%	22.2	3.7	40.8	27

Women are more likely than the men of broadcast news to have served as interns. That can be explained partially by women's being younger. Internships had become more prevalent by the time they went to college.

Minorities in TV have served internships at about the same rate as others. And though a number of stations have paid internships that are earmarked for their use, minority journalists are only slightly more likely than others to have served a paid internship. In radio, minorities are ex-interns more often than others, and the edge comes in paid internships.

Unpaid internships sometimes lead to paid ones. About half of the TV journalists who have held paid internships have also served the unpaid variety. This is consistent with the finding that, for every station with only paid internships, there's another with both kinds—where an intern can be promoted from unpaid one term to paid the next.

Playing by the Rules

For the station, paying or not paying makes a big difference. If paid, the intern is on the payroll and can work pretty much as regular staff, with all appropriate benefits and obligations. If unpaid, the intern must not be treated like regular staff or even an employee trainee. Else, the Fair Labor Standards Act (FLSA) requirements on minimum wage, overtime pay, etc. apply. To be exempt from FLSA rules governing an "employee," the unpaid student intern must meet *all* of the following criteria:

1. The training, even though it includes actual operation of the facilities of the employer, is similar to that which would be given in a vocational school.
2. The training is for the benefit of the trainees or students.
3. The trainees do not displace regular employees, but work under their close observation.
4. The employer that provides the training derives no immediate advantage from the activities of the trainees or students; and on occasion the employer's operations may actually be impeded.
5. The trainees or students are not necessarily entitled to a job at the conclusion of the training period.
6. The employer and the trainees or students understand that they are not entitled to wages for the time spent in training.[3]

While not necessary, formal college course credit for the internship can be seen as evidence that it's for the benefit of the student and that the intern is not being treated as an employee.

The provisions have been interpreted to mean that an intern should not be given work that might displace the work of a regular employee or otherwise benefit the employer.

If a station strictly meets the six FSLA criteria, an unpaid intern may tend to be little more than an observer or "gofer" (as in "go for" coffee) or "extra" doing things the newsroom could do without ("employer...derives no immediate advantage"). That's a far cry from the old paid internships at WTMJ TV and Radio, Milwaukee, where University of Wisconsin journalism students wrote, edited, reported and even went on the air. Unpaid interns no doubt still do these things in many of the stations without union employees, as is the case for most in small and middle markets. Some of these stations get by with violating wage and hour laws for regular staff—so why not for interns? But in major markets, unionized staff serve as watchdogs to protect their jobs from free labor, often leaving only a watered down experience for the unpaid intern.

Win-Win as the Goal

Helping in even a small way to get things done professionally in a major-market newsroom may be worth more than poorly supervised hands-on work in a bush-league shop. At least, that's the thinking of Tony Villasana, news operations director at KSDK-TV, St. Louis. One of his duties is to oversee an internship program that 380 students have completed since 1983. The interns are unpaid and must earn academic credit. As Villasana sees it:

> *The time each intern spends with us is a win-win situation for the student and the station. The intern is given the opportunity to learn from media professionals in a setting that's unavailable in many colleges and universities. The station, on the other hand, benefits from those services the intern performs.*
>
> *For example, even answering the phone at the assignment desk gives the intern the expe-*

rience of taking calls that might lead to a story. He or she learns what is potentially newsworthy and how to determine priorities and react accordingly.

Interns who do an outstanding job are often referred to news departments seeking entry level producers, reporters, etc. Interns whose performance is mediocre or marginal quickly learn that their chances of competing are not good. While it may be a bitter pill to swallow, it's an important one in deciding on a career.

The Television Sore Thumb

Valuable as unpaid internships may be, students working their way through school may not be able to make the financial sacrifice. And television stands out among the mass media as the one least likely to pay interns. Radio is a close second from last. In a 1990-91 survey of 1990 journalism and mass communication graduates, Lee Becker of Ohio State found that 64 percent of the internships served with daily newspapers were paid, compared to 20 percent for TV news. My 1991 TV survey showed only 9 percent paid. A possible explanation is that I surveyed news directors regarding all interns, whereas Becker surveyed communication graduates. For radio, Becker found 25 percent and I found 21 percent of all internships paid. His figures or mine, it matters little—TV and radio news are not in the same ballpark with daily newspapers.

Television and radio also trail other media occupations. Becker found that 51 percent of all internships were paid in public relations, 48 percent in advertising and 45 percent in magazines.[4]

Why are TV and radio news so far behind everyone else?

Worse off financially? Not television. Commercial TV stations are profitable, even in small markets.[5] Daily newspapers, magazines and radio stations fall to competition and go out of business. But network affiliated TV stations almost never fold—they're too busy making money.[6] Yet their internships carry pay only half as often as the ones in radio, where just staying in business is a challenge for many stations.[7]

More inclined to exploitation? We have certainly seen evidence that many stations pay news staff less than they would make in other media. Clearly less than TV stations can afford to pay. But other media have their robber barons, too. So that may or may not be the major factor.

Numbers? That appears the best explanation—the oversupply of students who want internships. Of course students want them. Half the people working in broadcast news today had them. They're tickets to jobs. And 20 percent of broadcasting programs not only recommend, but require internships (a practice many see as academically unsound).[8] So faculty and students come begging and stations hate to say no. Besides, many if not most news directors welcome opportunities to contribute to the education of their future fellow professionals.[9]

Greater use of paid internships for TV and radio news was suggested by the Roper Organization in reporting its 1987 survey of broadcast executives on the topic of higher education and career preparation. The study, commissioned by RTNDA, concluded that...

> ...internship programs, as they are currently organized, are not providing students with the types of experience which executives feel they need... One of the reasons for this may be that the overwhelming percentage of executives whose stations offer internships say these internships are unpaid...
>
> Given the large number of college students today who pay for their schooling through a combination of direct aid and work-study programs or other jobs outside of school, it may be that students cannot realistically afford to take

> *advantage of unpaid internship programs. This may be an area where the broadcast industry might have to reassess its own policies and procedures and make certain changes in order to achieve its objectives.*[10]

Reassessment is also in order for higher education. The academy bears at least as much responsibility as the industry, particularly for the surplus of students trying to get into the field. Faced with student numbers and limited campus facilities, educators have turned over a significant part of broadcast news education to the industry.

Leading educators are among those who have suggested that exploitation may be involved in internships that pay in academic credit instead of money and that "the academic unit is at least an accomplice in this exploitative system."[10] That may well be. But when working TV and radio journalists are in effect teaching hundreds of hours of course credits, for which faculty are paid, who's exploiting whom?

More paid internships are to be encouraged for accomplished students who can do a professional job that justifies wages. But at least half of the five thousand or so who are now in newsrooms probably have not reached that point in their development. For them, unpaid internships can make sense. These interns may make a financial sacrifice, as indeed they do to earn their other college credits. But, in return, many if not most gain a priceless opportunity to see broadcast journalism up close, to contribute what they can to a real-life news operation and perhaps to make career decisions. Such benefits may be worth far more than a few weeks or months on a minimum-wage payroll. And that internship, unpaid though it may be, looks good on a resume at job-hunting time.

CHAPTER 10

Staff Benefits

It's the total compensation package that counts. If you must pay for your health insurance, or even the greater part of it, knock a few hundred dollars off what you call your salary. If your employer contributes to a pension plan, add a few hundred—that's income for later use. Profit-sharing makes you part of the organization, as do bonuses based on how well the station does in the marketplace.

Staff benefits in broadcast news range from several thousand dollars a year invested in the typical employee by some stations to very little by others. Some stations contribute generously to health and life insurance plans and to retirement and pension funds, while offering liberal vacations, profit-sharing and bonuses for most news staff. Others, most notably radio stations in small markets, stop with base pay and legally required payments to Social Security. Staff benefits for full-time newspeople are sometimes as low as for part-time fast-food workers.

The trend in broadcasting, as in other industries, is to let the employee pick up more of the load. Though the findings summarized in most of this chapter's tables are from a 1987 study, surveys by the National Association of Broadcasters in 1991 for television and 1992 for radio enable trends comparisons across recent years.[1] Having aged through six years of cost-cutting, our data tend to err in favor of the employer.

The RTNDA-sponsored study reported here was done jointly with John Quarderer, a University of Missouri journalism faculty member who later joined the research department of Frank N. Magid Associates. Parts of this chapter are adapted from our initial report.[2]

Benefits and Trends

Employee Medical Insurance

The trend in the U.S. work force is for the employee to pay a bigger share of health insurance.[3] That goes for broadcasting. In 1987, more than half the responding TV news directors said their stations paid health and hospitalization premiums in full for their employees. Most others paid jointly with staff. But by 1991, an NAB survey found less soloing by the employer—the majority of TV stations contributed only jointly with staff.

In radio, also, the trend is for the staff member to pay more. Our 1987 survey found that 45 percent of the stations paid the full premium, a third paid part and a fifth paid none. Five years later, the NAB found less than a third of all radio stations paying the full tab, less than half sharing cost with employees and about half paying nothing.

A few stations have plans under which employees pay the total premium. That's not really a giant step removed from telling staff they're free to go out and buy their own health insurance. We'll line up a group rate, says the station, but you still pay the whole thing.

In small-markets, more than a third of the radio stations sampled let health/hospitalization insurance come totally from the pockets of their staff. This was less often the case in medium, large and major markets.

Dependents Medical Insurance

Most TV stations offer some kind of medical plan to cover employee's dependents, and the trend is toward cost-sharing. Half in our 1987 survey contributed jointly, a third left full payment to the employee and a sixth of the stations picked up the full tab for dependents as well as staff. In 1991, the NAB found cost-sharing by two-thirds.

TABLE 10.1: Who Pays for Employee Health Insurance

	All by Station	Paid Jointly	All by Staff	None	N
Television	56.0%	41.6	1.5	.9	327
Net Affiliates	56.1%	43.2	.4	.4	285
Independents	54.8%	31.0	9.5	4.8	42
1-25 Affils	40.0%	60.0	.0	.0	25
1-25 Indies	55.0%	40.0	5.0	.0	20
ADI 26-50	58.5%	34.1	4.9	2.4	41
ADI 51-100	54.3%	44.6	.0	1.1	92
ADI 101-150	64.0%	33.7	1.1	1.1	89
ADI 151-214	51.7%	46.7	1.7	.0	60
Radio	44.6%	35.2	8.7	11.4	332
Major Markets	53.2%	34.0	8.5	4.3	47
Large Markets	62.3%	34.4	1.6	1.6	61
Medium Markets	47.9%	37.0	6.7	8.4	119
Small Markets	26.7%	34.3	15.2	23.8	105

TABLE 10.2: Who Pays for Dependents' Health Insurance

	All by Station	Paid Jointly	All by Staff	None
Television	16.6%	50.0	32.2	1.3
Net Affiliates	16.7%	51.4	31.2	.7
Independents	15.8%	39.5	39.5	5.3
1-25 Affils	16.7%	66.7	16.7	.0
1-25 Indies	21.1%	42.1	36.8	.0
ADI 26-50	14.6%	31.7	51.2	2.4
ADI 51-100	15.6%	57.8	25.6	1.1
ADI 101-150	14.8%	43.2	40.9	1.1
ADI 151-214	20.7%	43.1	34.5	1.7
Radio	12.8%	35.3	31.1	20.8
Major Markets	25.6%	37.2	32.6	4.7
Large Markets	12.1%	39.7	39.7	8.6
Medium Markets	11.6%	32.1	33.0	23.2
Small Markets	9.1%	24.2	34.3	32.3

About half of the radio stations we surveyed in 1987 paid at least part of health insurance costs for dependents. But in small markets, contributing stations dropped to a third, with another third offering a plan paid in full by employees. The other third of the small-market radio stations had no plan for dependents.

The NAB's 1992 survey found that two of every five responding radio stations had some kind of cost-sharing plan for dependents' medical insurance.

Dental Insurance

The cost of insuring teeth and gums is also shifting to the employee. In 1987, the majority of TV stations in our survey were paying into dental insurance and picking up the full tab about as often as sharing costs. By 1991, the NAB survey showed the majority of stations still contributing, but less often paying the premiums in full.

TABLE 10.3: Who Pays for Dental Insurance

	All by Station	Paid Jointly	All by Staff	None
Television	29.4%	27.9	4.7	38.0
Net Affiliates	30.1%	28.5	3.6	37.8
Independents	25.0%	22.5	12.5	40.0
1-25 Affils	40.0%	36.0	4.0	20.0
1-25 Indies	25.0%	35.0	10.0	30.0
ADI 26-50	24.4%	34.1	7.3	34.1
ADI 51-100	34.8%	29.2	3.4	32.6
ADI 101-150	30.9%	20.2	6.0	42.9
ADI 151-214	19.3%	26.3	1.8	52.6
Radio	15.6%	13.6	8.6	62.3
Major Markets	28.3%	28.3	10.9	32.6
Large Markets	21.8%	21.8	7.3	49.1
Medium Markets	15.0%	8.4	3.7	72.9
Small Markets	6.4%	7.4	13.8	72.3

Radio newspeople seldom find dental insurance outside major or large markets. That's shown by our survey and the NAB's. Most stations in small and medium markets let staff worry about their own teeth.

Life Insurance

Employer-paid life insurance premiums are the single most likely benefit for TV news employees. Nearly two-thirds of the TV news directors told us their stations picked up those premiums in full. Even in the smallest TV markets, half of the stations paid the full cost of life insurance. In the lower tier of medium markets, three-fourths did.

TABLE 10.4: Who Pays for Life Insurance

	All by Station	Paid Jointly	All by Staff	None
Television	65.6%	22.1	4.4	7.9
Net Affiliates	67.1%	21.8	4.6	6.4
Independents	54.1%	24.3	2.7	18.9
1-25 Affils	62.5%	33.3	.0	4.2
1-25 Indies	68.4%	26.3	.0	5.3
ADI 26-50	65.0%	20.1	5.0	10.0
ADI 51-100	64.4%	27.8	6.7	1.1
ADI 101-150	76.5%	12.9	3.5	7.1
ADI 151-214	52.5%	22.0	5.1	20.3
Radio	39.6%	17.9	9.1	33.4
Major Markets	48.9%	26.7	11.1	13.3
Large Markets	57.9%	22.8	3.5	15.8
Medium Markets	36.3%	18.6	5.3	39.8
Small Markets	28.0%	9.7	16.1	46.2

In radio, employees at one out of three stations find no opportunity to buy any life insurance through their employers. In small markets, only about one of three radio stations were contributing to life insurance.

No trend is apparent regarding life insurance. NAB surveys in the early 1990s showed about the same as ours for television and a little higher station participation than ours for radio.

Basic term life insurance, of course, is not terribly expensive for people in their 20s and 30s, as most in broadcast news are. It's a drop in the bucket compared to health insurance.

Retirement/Pension Plans

Nearly two-thirds of the TV news directors in our 1987 survey said their stations offered some type of retirement or pension plan. About one of every five stations made the full contribution. A fourth said there was a retirement plan but did not say who paid for it.

TABLE 10.5: Who Pays for Retirement/Pension Plans

	All by Station	Paid Jointly	Unspecified	All by Staff	None
Television	18.8%	15.4	26.6	3.4	35.7
Net Affiliates	20.1%	16.2	28.1	3.6	32.0
Independents	9.8%	9.8	17.1	2.4	61.0
1-25 Affils	25.0%	12.5	54.2	.0	8.3
1-25 Indies	10.0%	20.0	25.0	.0	45.0
ADI 26-50	31.7%	7.3	29.3	4.9	26.8
ADI 51-100	15.6%	22.2	33.3	4.4	24.4
ADI 101-150	19.3%	14.8	19.3	3.4	43.2
ADI 151-214	14.3%	10.7	14.3	3.6	57.1
Radio	5.5%	2.5	6.8	3.1	82.2
Major Markets	18.2%	6.8	18.2	9.1	47.7
Large Markets	10.2%	5.1	13.6	3.4	67.8
Medium Markets	2.6%	.9	5.2	1.7	89.7
Small Markets	.9%	.9	.0	1.9	96.2

The larger the news operation, the more likely was there to be a retirement/pension plan. Almost no operations with news staffs of 36 or more lacked such plans, but two-thirds of the TV news staffs of 10 or fewer were without them.

While our survey did not differentiate between pension plans and 401(k) plans, the 1991 survey by NAB did. It found that more than a third of TV stations paid pension plans in full and more than half paid nothing at all. But half did contribute jointly to 401(k) plans, with only a third not offering them. The 401(k) is growing in popularity.[4]

Most radio employees outside the larger markets can get along on Social Security and IRAs as far as their stations are concerned. About half of the ones we surveyed in major markets and a third in large markets had retirement plans of some kind. But most in small and medium markets offered neither pension nor 401(k) plans.

NAB findings for radio five years later differed little from ours.

Profit-Sharing

A third of the TV and a sixth of the radio stations in the 1987 survey had profit-sharing plans for employees. Profit-sharing was as prevalent in the smallest TV markets as in others. But in radio, it was rarely reported in small markets. Findings in NAB surveys in the early 1990s were generally quite similar to ours.

TABLE 10.6: Stations with Profit-Sharing and Bonus Plans

	Profit-Sharing	Bonus Plans
Television	34.4%	43.7%
Net Affiliates	36.6%	46.1%
Independents	17.6%	26.4%
1-25 Affils	31.8%	54.6%
1-25 Indies	29.4%	23.5%
ADI 26-50	29.7%	54.0%
ADI 51-100	38.8%	43.8%
ADI 101-150	30.8%	46.2%
ADI 151-214	38.9%	35.2%
Radio	15.2%	35.2%
Major Markets	18.2%	45.5%
Large Markets	22.4%	39.7%
Medium Markets	15.6%	33.0%
Small Markets	8.6%	30.1%

Bonuses

Broadcast news employees may earn bonuses at a fair number of stations. Two of every five TV news directors and a third of the radio news directors told us their stations offered bonuses. Both in television and radio, bonuses were somewhat more likely to be had in larger operations.

TV Benefits Package Examples

The bottom line for the employee is the total package of benefits. Examples, which show how benefits tend to get smaller with the size of the market or staff:

An award-winning TV network affiliate with a news staff of 90 in an ADI 1-25 market was paying employee health and dental insurance premiums in full. The station and employees jointly paid for health insurance for dependents, life insurance and a retirement plan. Bonuses were paid. Vacations were two weeks after one year and three weeks after five.

An ADI 11-25 network affiliate with 59 news employees was paying life and dental premiums in full. Employees paid part of their health insurance and the full premiums for a dependents health policy. Joint contributions went into a retirement plan. Profit-sharing and bonuses were in place. Vacations were two weeks after one year, three weeks after five.

A medium-market station with 42 newspeople paid employee health and life insurance premiums in full, but premiums for dependents health insurance were paid fully by employees. No dental plan. Joint payments for a retirement plan. No profit-sharing. No bonuses. Vacations were two weeks after one year, three weeks after seven.

A TV station just outside the top 100 markets paid individual health, dependent health and life insurance jointly with its 28 news staff. There was no dental plan. No profit-sharing. No bonuses. The station paid into retirement. Vacations were two weeks after one year, three weeks after five.

A TV station in one of the nation's smallest markets contributed to individual and dependents health insurance jointly with its nine full-time news employees. There was no dental insurance. No retirement plan. No bonuses or profit-sharing. Two weeks of vacation a year, with no increase.

Radio Package Examples

A model benefits package was reported by an FM radio station with five full-time newspeople in a major market. The station paid individual and dependents health insurance, dental insurance, life insurance and retirement contributions in full. There was a profit-sharing plan but no bonuses for news staff. Vacations are three weeks after one year, four weeks after five. The same person has been news director 12 years.

A well known old major-market AM station had essentially those same benefits and a news director who had been in the job 14 years and was making $52,000 a year.

The one-woman news staff of a large-market FM station got her health insurance, life insurance and retirement (8 percent of salary) paid in full by the station, which would pay for health insurance for dependents if she had any. Profit-sharing and bonuses were offered. Vacations were two weeks after one year, three weeks after two.

A medium-market AM-FM operation with distinguished call letters had a similar package. And vacations never got longer than two weeks.

At a fairly typical small-market radio station, the one full-time newsperson had his basic health insurance paid by the station, but that's all. Nothing for dependents, dental, life or retirement. No profit-sharing or bonuses. Never more than one week of vacation per year. If he wanted benefits, he was free to buy them himself with what was left after taxes on his salary of $10,400.

But he was still doing better than the woman making $9,900 after seven years as an AM/FM news director in Kentucky. Her employer didn't even offer a health insurance plan, only life insurance and an occasional bonus in lieu of a raise. If she got pregnant, she would be on her own and probably out of a job.

Maternity Benefits

Most TV stations and two-thirds of commercial radio stations offer maternity leave with an equivalent job assured upon a woman's return. TV stations are more likely than radio to pay all or part of her salary during the leave, which typically is for upward of eight weeks.

Those findings are from my 1990 multi-topic survey of news directors. They were first reported in an article co-authored by Kimberly K. Burks, a research assistant who went from her master's degree to a job as news producer at WHBQ-TV, Memphis.[5]

Most of the women working in broadcast news are of typical child-bearing age—early 20s through early 40s. Nearly a third of them already have young children.

As Table 10.7 shows, women in television are more likely than those in radio to be able to take a maternity leave and have their jobs held for them. At least, that was the case in the early 1990s at nine out of 10 TV stations, but just two of every three radio stations.

Nearly half the radio stations said the woman was paid nothing while on leave, and she got only part of her regular salary at most others. But in television, only a fifth paid nothing—a third paid her full salary during the leave. At half of the radio and TV stations paying maternity leave, it went beyond regular medical leave.

How long does paid maternity leave last? Typically for five to eight weeks. About a fourth of the stations limit it to a month or less. Few pay for longer than eight weeks.

In TV newsrooms, the larger the staff size, the better the maternity benefits. In the smallest newsrooms (10 or fewer full-timers), 40 percent of the stations were paying nothing. But among stations with the largest news staffs (36 or more), only 5 percent paid nothing. A woman's full salary was paid during maternity leave at half of the stations with 21 or more newspeople, but at only a fourth with smaller news staffs.

TABLE 10.7: Stations Providing Family Benefits

	TV	Radio
Maternity leave	90.1%	66.3%
Station pays no salary	20.8%	44.6%
Station pays part	42.5	45.4
Station pays all	36.6	10.0
1–4 weeks paid	22.3%	27.8%
5-8 weeks paid	58.5	53.7
9–22 weeks paid	13.3	11.2
Depends	5.8	7.3
Beyond regular medical	48.9%	50.0%
Comparable for fathers	8.9%	7.7%
Help with child care	1.9%	1.3%
Child-care tax benefits	19.6%	5.7%
Flex-time for family needs	60.2%	77.2%
EAP counseling	35.5%	13.2%
N	416	276

TV stations with larger staffs are somewhat more likely than others to pay for more than eight weeks of leave.

In radio, where most news staffs are small, the relationship between staff size and family benefits is not as clear as in television. But, again, the larger operations tend to have better benefits. At those many stations with only one full-time newsperson, the majority offer maternity leave but only half of those pay the woman any salary while she's gone. At radio stations with two or more full-timers in news, two-thirds offer maternity leave and two-thirds of those pay at least part of salary during the leave.

Other Family Benefits

What about comparable leave for fathers? As Table 10.7 shows, it was available at only a handful of stations in 1990, and about as rare in large operations as in small.

Child care is totally up to the parents as far as most stations are concerned. Less than a handful of news directors in either radio or television said their stations provided or subsidized child care for employees. Even among the largest operations, only 4 percent of TV and 5 percent of radio stations were offering any child-care help.

Pre-tax salary reductions for child care were available through 20 percent of the TV and 6 percent of the radio stations surveyed. A third of the TV stations with news staffs of 36 or more offered such pre-tax salary reductions.

Flex-time for family needs was available in the majority of TV and radio newsrooms. They allow some flexibility to let a person leave for important family matters, but not much. Only 3 percent of the TV and 8 percent of the radio NDs checked "much" rather than "some" flex-time. This flexibility of hours is found least often in the largest TV newsrooms.

Employment Assistance Programs providing counseling for health, family and financial problems were in effect at a third of the TV stations but very few radio stations. The share of stations with EAP counseling ranged from 9 percent of radio stations with no more than one full-time newsperson to 61 percent of TV stations with news staffs of 36 or more.

The Federal Family and Medical Leave Act of 1993 applies to many stations, but many others—those with less than 50 workers—are exempt. The great majority of radio stations and most of the really small-market (ADI 150-210) TV stations have well under 50 employees. So do many TV stations in middle markets and some of the independents in major markets.

The 1993 law says workers in non-exempt firms are entitled to up to a total of 12 weeks of unpaid leave during any 12-month period for: the birth of a child or an adoption; need to care for a child, spouse or parent with a serious health condition; or their own serious health condition that makes them unable to perform their job. Employers must continue to provide health-care benefits during the unpaid leave.

The Family and Medical Leave Act covers only workers who have been employed for at least one year and for at least 1,250 hours, an average of 25 hours a week.

Companies may deny the benefit to salaried employees within the highest paid 10 percent of their work force if letting the workers take the leave would create "substantial and grievous injury" to the business operations. Sweeps periods could be bad times for high paid anchors to ask for family leave.

Assessing Benefits

Staff benefits in broadcast news vary widely, even among comparable stations. On average, the larger the operation, the more generous the benefits. But some prominent TV stations in major markets give their employees as little as they can get by with, while a few small-market radio stations add what amounts to a fourth or more to "real" salaries through first-rate benefits packages.

Health insurance and retirement plans are expensive. For example, staff benefits add roughly 25 percent to dollars in payroll costs at the University of Missouri.[6] That's just the start. Add vacations, holidays and other "payment for time not worked," and the U. S. Chamber of Commerce calculates that total benefits typically cost employers 37 percent beyond salaries.[7]

But that's another world for the stations that don't pay benefits. These are the same stations that pay poverty wages. So the newspeople who can least afford it are the ones most often left to shift for themselves on health insurance, pension plans and other staff benefits.

CHAPTER 11

Bottom and Top

Television news has its salary extremes. High enough for incentive. Low enough to discourage some of the many potential newcomers. Five percent of all TV newspeople in the 1990-91 careers survey were making $100,000 or more, good pay even with the high cost of living in a major market. Five percent were below $14,000.

Let's put aside the medians, the averages, the often dull rank and file. And look at newspeople who have made it big or definitely have not. How do they differ? What stands out for the ones in the Hundred Grand Club? What lessons may their stories hold for the young journalist who's now at the bottom but aspires to the top?

How They Differ

It's no surprise that TV journalists who earn $100,000 or more are older—42 on average vs. 24 for the ones below $14,000. The lowest paid are most often young beginners.

TABLE 11.1: The Bottom and Top 5 Percent in TV News Salaries

	Less than $14,000	$100,000 and up
Median age	24	42
Male	50.0%	77.2%
White	94.8%	88.6%
In ADI 1–25	9.0%	73.1%
In ADI 26–50	7.7%	17.9%
Median staff size	21	74
Present job:		
Photographer	32.5%	0%
Reporter	23.4	15.2
Producer	13.0	3.8
Anchor	11.7	49.4
News director	.0	8.9
Median years in news	2	18
Jobs held	2	5
Years on present job	1	11
Hours worked weekly	45	51
Married	23.1%	82.1%
Married to earner	81.0%	42.9%
Earn more than spouse	33.3%	94.6%
College graduates	83.3%	87.3%
J-Mass Comm majors	88.6%	55.4%
Most valuable course:		
Writing	31.9%	39.4%
TV hands-on	37.6	16.4
Social studies	10.1	19.7
Wish more of:		
Writing	27.8%	10.2%
TV hands-on	18.5	4.0
Social studies	16.7	42.9
Business	7.4	16.3
N	78	79

About half of all entry-level hires are now women, as are half of the lowest paid TV news staff. Men outnumber women three to one among the highest paid—that goes with their big lead in age and experience.

Minorities are more likely to be among the top-paid than bottom-paid. They work predominantly in larger markets, where pay is higher.

Most TV journalists who make $100,000 or more work in the 50 largest markets. Three-fourths are in ADI 1-25.

Their poor cousins are spread across markets of all sizes. One of every six who makes less than $14,000 does so in an ADI 1-50 market. But most are found in middle and small markets—30 percent in ADI 51-100, 19 percent in 101-150 and 35 percent in 151-210. Only about a third of the lowest paid are in the smallest markets, as conventional wisdom would suggest. But then, contrary to such wisdom, surveys show that new college graduates are hired in markets of all sizes.

Top money-makers are normally found in large operations, in news staffs averaging 74. The median Big Three network affiliate in the 25 largest markets in 1992 employed 79 full-time news staff. The median in the 60 smallest markets was 13. The median staff size for newspeople making under $14,000 was 21, about the same as the median of 22 for all stations. Again, the highest paid are found mainly in big-time newsrooms, but the lowest paid may show up anywhere.

And what are they doing? The top-paid are anchors in half the cases. They're next most likely to be reporters in major markets or news directors. The bottom-paid are most often photographers or reporters. Producers and (surprise?) anchors also count as cellar occupants quite often.

The highest paid TV journalists have settled in—typically in their present jobs for 14 years, with four earlier jobs and a total of 18 years in the field. The lowest paid average about one year in their present jobs, plus a year on an earlier one, as one might expect for a 24-year-old.

The top money-makers work longer hours than the bottom earners—51 vs. 45 hours a week. But they're usually on contracts that do not allow pay for overtime. Beginning reporters and photographers, on the other hand, are most often eligible to be paid time and a half for all hours over 40 and must limit their overtime.

Being older, the top-paid are more likely to be married. And being more affluent, they are less likely to have spouses who hold full-time paying jobs. A husband can keep house and play golf when the anchorwoman earns $135,000. But when she brings in only $13,500, they both have to work.

Question: "Who earns more—you or your spouse?" Among the top-paid, it's almost always the TV journalist. Among the bottom-paid, it's the spouse in two-thirds of the cases.

Education levels are about the same for the bottom and top earners. Most are college graduates.

Those at the bottom are more likely to have majored in one of the many varieties of journalism and mass communication. A majority of the top-paid also have JMC majors. But more often than the bottom-paid, they majored in social studies, English or another liberal arts area.[1]

"What single course in college has helped you most?" Differences are not great, but the top-paid most often say writing, while the bottom-paid cite hands-on training in TV news. The top-paid are twice as likely to say a course in social studies has helped them most. (Labor economics proved the most valuable for my broadcast news work in 1950s and '60s Louisville, where few months passed without a strike or the threat of one.)

"Of courses you didn't take, which do you wish most you had?" More social studies (history, political science, sociology, etc.), say the journalists making $100,000 or more. In their many years of news work, they have found they can never learn enough about the topics of the news. Next are business courses, of particular value to the news director charged with running a profit-center. Respondents making under $14,000 most often say they would take more writing. Some learned how to report and produce slick "packages" but skipped the less glamorous how-to-write, and now they wish they hadn't. Still, sizable numbers of the lowest paid wish they had taken more hands-on—some of their schools offered none. And about as many wish they had taken more social studies.

The successful veterans send a message to college students with an eye toward TV news careers. For long-term success, give top priority to writing and courses in fields like social studies that educate you in the substance of news. Don't let liberal arts education be crowded out by excessive time on TV skills courses. In the short term, they're great for resume tapes and entry-level jobs in small markets. But for moving to the top, the courses that help most are the ones that help you become a truly literate and educated person.

Their Views and Plans

The best paid TV journalists, not surprisingly, are happier in their jobs than are the worst-paid. When asked their "overall job satisfaction," a fourth of the best-paid but practically none of the worst-paid checked "very satisfied." Still, fully two-thirds of the worst-paid said they were at least "satisfied." Not quite a third were dissatisfied. Fourteen percent of the best-paid also said they were dissatisfied.

The worst-paid are no more likely than the best-paid to be thinking of getting out. In both groups, fewer than half said yes when asked: "Have you seriously considered leaving broadcast news?" The best-paid had made it and were happy. The worst-paid were mostly young people looking to better years ahead.

"If you got out of broadcast news, what do you think would be the main reason? "Pay" was checked by two-thirds of the respondents making less than $14,000. "Lack of advancement" was second. (Multiple responses were accepted.) Those making $100,000 or more have already achieved pay and advancement. Their main reasons for getting out would be "family life" and "disenchantment with the field."

Disenchantment? Yes. TV news is exciting and fun. And it can pay well. But it can also wear thin. The crime stories, sweeps periods, promotions and anchor hairdos all begin to look alike. And one day you may contemplate the profit center and ask—is that all there is?

But that's not the kind of disenchantment we'd expect from the third of the worst-paid who said it might drive them out.

Most are too young to be jaded by time. Their disenchantment more likely relates to pay.

TABLE 11.2: The Bottom and Top 5 Percent in Pay Look to the Future

	Less than $14,000	$100,000 and up
Job satisfaction:		
Very satisfied	1.4%	24.4%
Satisfied	68.9	61.5
Dissatisfied	23.0	12.8
Very dissatisfied	6.8	1.3
Might leave TV news	45.3%	45.5%
Might go for:		
Better pay	67.9%	6.3%
Prof. advancement	42.6	10.1
Less stress	38.5	35.4
Family reasons	30.8	40.5
Disenchantment	34.6	38.0
Open to better job in distant city	88.5%	57.7%

Stress also drives TV newspeople to other occupations. More than a third of the best paid, the worst paid and those between say stress might send them packing. There's no escaping it. Stress is everywhere—in deadlines, ratings and lack of feedback on job performance. It can be stimulating or destructive. If you can cope with stress, fine. Otherwise, you may want to dump the ulcers or migraines for a less glamorous job.

"If you were offered a much better job that required you to move to a distant city, do you think you would accept it?" Most of the lowest-paid and more than half of the highest-paid TV journalists in the careers survey checked "yes." Mobility is usually necessary for moving to the top.

Some at the Top

The highest paid respondent in the careers survey—an anchorman making $1.8 million—didn't wait for the world to come to him. As a freshman in college, he went job-hunting at the local NBC affiliate and wound up working nights as a reporter/anchor for the four years it took to complete a communication major. Four years and two steppingstone jobs later, he was in one of the three largest markets at a station where he had been working for 17 years at the time of the survey. Salary, challenge and autonomy are very important to him, but he says the glamour of the job is not. He has not considered getting out of TV news. But if he did, it would be because the job often interferes with his home life. He works 50-60 hours a week. If he got out, he would probably write novels.

A 34-year-old anchorwoman earning $275,000 in an ADI 11-25 market has been at her station eight years and aspires to a larger market and better pay. She majored in theatre and psychology and says courses in writing and public speaking have helped her most. Autonomy, excitement and glamour in the job are only fairly important. Salary is very important. The worst thing about her present job is that it disrupts her personal life. She's a wife and mother, with a babysitter doing most of the child care. She'd like to teach, except for the pay.

At 30, a woman who anchors and reports for an ADI 1-10 station makes $150,000, which is more than she expected back when she was majoring in broadcast journalism and political science and working as an unpaid intern. She loves her station and stays on though confident she could make it with a major network. But all is not well. She works 60 hours a week in "a horrible schedule that conflicts with that of my spouse." They're now separated, and she's having stress-related health problems. She also feels a "desire to try something that would be more rewarding to society." She has thought of becoming a veterinarian.

A 42-year-old anchorwoman in ADI 26-50 has cut back to 35 hours a week for family reasons. She makes $125,000, which is more than she thought lay ahead when she got her degree in speech and English 22 years ago. The demands of the job put sometimes "debilitating" stress on her as a wife and mother. She would like to become a talk show host.

An anchorman in one of the top 10 markets is making $650,000 after 26 years in the field. He majored in political science and English, then added a master's in journalism. Writing courses have helped him most, and he wishes he had taken more history. He's been in his present job 12 years and says it will be his last as a TV anchor. He works 65-70 hours a week, has long anchored the late news, and says "working nights is very difficult for a family while children are growing up." Upon retiring as an anchor, he hopes to get into TV and radio syndication and write books and articles.

A meterorologist/environmental anchor in ADI 11-25 is making $275,000 just 11 years out of school with a degree in meteorology. But part of that is from a company he has launched on the side to syndicate weather information and sell new computer graphics software. He's thinking of getting out of TV news. It's disruptive of family life. And he's tired of being "a hostage of TV management." He wants to "call my own shots."

Disenchantment is also expressed by a major-market reporter who makes $160,000, about what she expected by now when she graduated in journalism 20 years ago. She blames the hours she had to work for ending her first marriage. But more stress now comes from the "unhealthy climate and hostile environment at work since the profit mentality took over." She's looking to retirement to work at home as a writer of articles and books.

On the management track, a woman who earns $126,000 as news director with a staff of 100 in an ADI 1-10 market reports no marital or health problems related to the job. She works 60 hours a week, earns more than her husband and leaves child care to a nanny. In college, 18 years ago, she majored in communication and government. Her favorite was government. And though she's not seriously considering getting out of broadcast news, she's open to exploring other areas, possibly "something in policy regarding politics and the press."

A news director who's 61 and earning $180,000 in one of the three largest markets still likes working in TV news. He puts in

50-55 hours a week. Looking back across the years since he earned a BS in journalism and MA in political science, he says he "possibly spent too much time on the job and too little at home with the wife and kids."

An assistant news director, also in a top-three market, makes well over $100,000 and aspires to become a news director and earn more. It has been 16 years since she earned a degree in history. She works 63 hours a week but still finds time for her daughter and husband.

All 10 of these examples of the best-paid were married at the time of the survey. Six had seen previous marriages end in divorce, and another was separated. The hours and demands of TV news drew much of the blame for relationships gone wrong.

Some at the Bottom

Most of the following examples from the survey's lowest paid were 22 to 25 years old.

An anchorwoman/reporter earning $13,000 at a large-market independent station with a small news staff is unhappy with the pay and stress. She's not doing as well as she expected when getting her broadcast journalism degree three years ago. But she's still determined to work her way up to a network job.

An anchorwoman/reporter making $11,000 in a small market three years after her degree in political science has a long-term eye on ADI 1-10. But her husband is the primary earner, and they face the problem of "who's going to move for career."

A graduate in comparative literature (history courses have helped her most) is making $9,600 after four months on a job as anchorwoman/reporter. She's disenchanted with "uneducated broadcast journalists who act irresponsibly" and is thinking of moving to print.

An anchorman/reporter one year from his broadcasting degree is making $10,000 a year for 50 hours a week. He's paying dues to become a sports or news anchor in a major market. His wife, who also works but makes even less in their small market, "sometimes gets angry that I work too much."

At $13,000 in a middle market one year after his communications degree, an unmarried reporter who aspires to ADI 1-10 anchoring realizes the early years can be lean. But, he writes, "I hate being poor!"

With similar aspirations, a woman who got her journalism degree four years ago, is making $13,500 as a reporter in a middle market. She says writing is proving her most valuable college course.

A sports producer/reporter making $12,000 as a part-timer in a large market has been told he must work more than the 20 hours he's paid for if he hopes to advance. Three years after a broadcast journalism degree, he says an internship has helped him most.

A small-market reporter making $13,000 in her first year after majoring in mass communication hopes eventually to become an anchor in a top-25 market. Just now, she's having trouble with backaches from carrying photographic equipment. **Back problems were reported by more than a third of the photographers and one-person-band reporters.**

A broadcast journalism major who's been out of school three years aspires to TV photojournalism in a top-10 market. For now, he's practicing it in a small market at $11,000. He's married and his wife also works, but he says they "are unable to have the standard of life we would like."

A small-market videographer who suffers backaches from lugging equipment gets only $10,900 for it. But what bothers him more is that "less competent fluff heads" are paid so much more for on-air jobs. Two years from majoring in accounting and TV/radio, he's looking for a job as an anchor.

A small-market assignment editor/reporter/anchor who got her degree in broadcast journalism a year ago is paying dues to become a reporter in a top-20 market someday. For now, 60 hours a week and $11,200 a year.

A hopeful Cinderella, an 11-year anchor/reporter, is free-lancing for as little as $10,000 a year in a top-10 market she says exploits freelancers. Her station employs eight full-time reporters/

anchors and calls in five "temps" as needed. She made big money and won awards in other major markets before moving to this one for family reasons. Now she's learning what it's like to freelance—"no benefits, no overtime, not more than 1,000 hours a year or we'd be eligible for pension. It's an abuse of people." Regular anchors at the station typically make $100,000 or more. With her track record, she believes the odds are good she'll soon be one of them. If the wand is waved, she could go all the way from a poverty level salary to $100,000-plus in just one day.

CHAPTER 12

Looking to 2000

Marketplace forces, most notably supply and demand, can be expected to determine pay levels for broadcast news in the future, as in the past. Thanks to surveys dating back 20 years, we're able to identify trends and, as in Chapter 5, to project salaries for the year 2000 as they'll be if the trends of the most recent five years continue. But trends level off. Or even change directions, often unpredictably.

For looking ahead, numbers from the past are not enough. Opinions of experts are needed to interpret the numbers and look to the future. This chapter draws primarily upon people who work in broadcast news daily, its news directors. In a 1990 survey, hundreds told of changes they expect to see during the last decade of the century. Then in 1993, working journalists who read drafts of chapters of this book joined me in assessing past and future trends.

News Directors Look Across the '90s

The 1990 RTNDA-sponsored survey asked news directors: "Looking ahead through the 1990s, what do you expect to change in your news operation?" Several newsroom variables were listed. For each, the respondents indicated their expectations by checking "more," "less" or "about the same."

Television

Production emphasis tops the list of things TV news directors expect "more" of in their newsrooms. As Table 12.1 shows, roughly three of every four news directors foresaw more emphasis on production across the 1990s. Will this mean higher pay for producers?

TABLE 12.1: How TV News Directors Expect Their Operations to Change During the 1990s

	More	About Same	Less
Production Emphasis	72.5%	23.8	3.7
Amount of Local Reporting	71.0%	27.4	1.6
Computerization	68.9%	30.4	.7
Air Time for News	68.7%	29.5	1.8
Newsroom Run as Profit Center	63.3%	34.7	2.1
Live Reports from News Scene	59.7%	39.3	.0
News Staff Size	52.2%	40.0	7.8
Spotlight on Anchors/Reporters	47.4%	46.2	6.4
Salaries Pacing Cost of Living	27.8%	54.7	17.5
Station's Share of Benefits Cost	20.8%	57.3	22.0

Number of Cases = 435

More local reporting came in next. A hopeful sign for reporters?

More computerization. Less demand and pay for staff who perform routine tasks?

More air time for news, confirmed in a 1992 survey.[1] Added dollars for salaries?

More running of the newsroom as a profit center. Holding down pay where possible?

More live reports from news scenes. Higher pay for reporters and photographers who are good at it?

Larger news staffs. Salary budgets to match? Or just more people earning less?

Spotlighting of anchors/reporters—more of it, or about the same as now. Those were the responses, and in roughly equal numbers. Very few think anchors and reporters will be downplayed. Does spotlighting mean higher pay?

How will salaries do at keeping up with the cost of living? Half said they expect things to go on pretty much as usual through the '90s. Among those expecting change, optimists outnumbered pessimists.

Stations' shares of staff benefits costs were also most often expected to stay about the same. One in five respondents looked ahead to their stations paying less of the tab, and one in five expected them to pay more.

Radio

Radio news directors most often expected things to go on pretty much as usual through the last decade of the 20th century. As Table 12.2 shows, the only thing on the survey's list that the majority see going up is computerization.

But substantial numbers expect upswings in local reporting, live reports from news scenes and specialized reporting and segments. All of these suggest a premium for first-hand reporting in radio news.

Profit-orientation is expected to remain at about the 1990

level in half of the radio newsrooms, but to loom larger in a third. While lower than for television, these figures leave no doubt that radio news directors expect to be held accountable for news that makes money.

TABLE 12.2: How Radio News Directors Expect Their Operations to Change During the 1990s

	More	About Same	Less
Computerization	59.9%	37.0	3.1
Amount of Local Reporting	42.8%	52.5	4.7
Live Reports from News Scene	40.6%	52.2	7.2
Specialized Reporting/Segments	39.3%	55.5	5.2
Newsroom Run as Profit Center	37.4%	54.6	8.0
Salaries Pacing Cost of Living	28.5%	52.0	19.4
News Staff Size	25.1%	68.1	6.0
Air Time for News	24.6%	67.7	7.6
Station's Share of Benefits Cost	18.3%	65.2	16.6
Spotlight on Anchors/Reporters	15.6%	73.2	11.3

Number of Cases = 340

Radio news salaries are most often expected to go on about the same, which means not keeping up with the Consumer Price Index. One of every five news directors expected the pace of pay in purchasing power to pick up. But another one in five looked sadly to further loss to inflation.

Radio stations' shares of such benefits as health insurance were seen as staying about the same, which generally means low.

Two-thirds expected no change in staff sizes. One in four looked for growth. In 1990, almost none thought there would be staff cuts. But cuts came, anyway. Surveys found radio news staffs getting smaller both in 1991 and 1992.[2]

Radio is expected to give "about the same" or "more" air time to news programming across the 1990s. Early in the decade, it increased.[3]

Thoughts on the Future

The public's appetite for news will remain as strong as ever in 2000 and beyond. But in an ever more competitive setting, the suppliers of news by radio and television can be expected to change. Let's assess some of the trends documented in this book.

Oversupply and Underpay

Low salaries, particularly in small markets, most often stem from 1) an oversupply of aspiring journalists who take jobs more for experience than for money and 2), in some markets, an oversupply of news operations, more than the local economy can support.

"It's a buyer's market," according to Gary Hanson, news director at WKBN-TV, Youngstown, Ohio, and 1992-93 RTNDA chairman. "The marketplace continues to be flooded with college graduates eager to start for little or no money."

Even before the economic crunch of the early 1990s, my research showed twice as many prospective new broadcast journalists as there were jobs for them. They'll work for low pay, and that's fine with the stations. In addition, hundreds of unpaid student interns work for experience. Federal regulations to the contrary, interns often serve as free labor, thus reducing demand and salaries for regular staff.

Little change is to be expected. Broadcast news is an attractive field, as those now practicing it told me in a careers survey. Don't look for a shortage of entry-level applicants for low-paying jobs.

Some markets may also have an oversupply of news operations. We know what happens when there's not enough of the advertising pie to go around. Somebody drops out. Across the 20th century, second and third newspapers in many cities failed. As we approach the 21st century, upward of two-thirds of all households subscribe to cable and its many channels, competing for the audiences that once loyally watched local news.

Lee Giles, news director at WISH-TV, Indianapolis, looks ahead: "For many stations, the economic base is shrinking in the face of competition. In the future, the year 2000, give or take a few years, we may well see a TV station or two in a given market cut back or eliminate news departments. The dominant stations in those markets will, at the same time, grow and continue to expand as the stations for local news."

One reason newspapers pay better for most news jobs than do television and radio may be the sounder economic base that comes from less competition. The typical city now has only one daily newspaper, but most TV markets have at least three stations competing for the local news audience. For now.

If low pay fosters low quality and eventual audience defection, many stations are only postponing a day of reckoning. In small markets, salaries for reporters and producers have not only failed to keep up with inflation, but have actually been going down. Even TV anchors and radio news directors sometimes show up below poverty level. This suggests marginal operations.

Lee Hall, news director, WSB Radio, Atlanta, observes that "shops in smaller markets, both radio and TV, are struggling," and some are closing.

Fallout From Small Markets

When underfinanced newsrooms pay too little to attract and hold high quality staff, more successful operations may also suffer.

"We have lost our farm system," Hall says. "Recruiting qualified anchors/reporters/producers from smaller markets has become increasingly difficult. When I speak to college classes, I find virtually no one with radio as a long-term career choice. As the salary picture worsens, we who require 'fresh blood' to fill our vacancies have a tougher time."

Emily Rooney, executive producer, ABC "World News Tonight," looks at the trends data and asks, "Are we degrading our business with the low salaries we offer in small markets?"

Yes. And probably driving some of our best prospective

broadcast journalists to better paying fields. For example, to newspaper, where they can do the reporting that local TV stations set to video the next evening. Staff come cheap in small markets—supply and demand. But another old principle is often at work, too, namely—you get what you pay for.

The clear danger to stations with first-rate news operations is that, if the pay in small and middle markets doesn't improve, the really talented prospects may be driven to other fields.

Underpaid Rank and File

The underpinning of broadcast news will also be endangered if salaries for the majority of news staff keep losing to inflation. Yes, newsroom managers and anchors in television have been keeping up. But not TV reporters, photographers and producers or most radio newspeople. And these are the basic news handlers, the staff who make it all possible.

WKBN-TV's Gary Hanson is concerned "that the people who make the major daily news decisions in newsrooms, producers and assignment editors, are among the lower paid. The industry needs to continue to attract bright, energetic and well educated people to those important positions."

Producers may find better days ahead. WISH-TV's Lee Giles believes they'll do better in the '90s than indicated by projections based on 1987-92 salaries. He says he finds stations "continually searching for qualified producers and finding the supply very limited. At the same time, stations are expanding or adding newscasts, and the demand is for ever more sophisticated newscasts in terms of pacing, content, graphics, live elements and such. I believe these factors, coupled with changing priorities, mean a very bright future for producers who excel."

That's supported by the survey in which TV news directors put "production emphasis" number one when asked which of several elements of their news operations would increase during the 1990s. Good producers will remain in demand, and be paid reasonably well in the 50 largest markets, as now. But will there be enough of those "who excel"? How many will have been driven from the pipeline by the low pay in smaller markets?

Reporters, on the other hand, may not do so well. Giles expects a leveling of reporters' salaries in larger markets. In small markets, they have already not only leveled but turned downward.

Photographers will probably remain at the bottom of the TV news pay charts. Whether the blame lies with technology or changing news priorities, the shooters of today are valued less than the photojournalists of old.

Anchors and Managers

"Anchors who recruit viewers and impact station image and ratings will do well," Giles predicts. "But leveling rather than escalation will be the rule for most."

Managers' prospects look good. With ever increasing emphasis on news as a profit-maker, Giles expects salaries to continue to go up for superior newsroom managers. He explains, "A station has too much at stake, with both the profit margin and its image, not to have bright, talented people running its number one priority, the news department."

Giles, who has headed the WISH-TV news department for 25 years, looks toward 2000 and sees news directors' salaries continuing to outpace inflation in medium to major markets. "That's commensurate with the tremendously growing pressures and responsibilities of managing complex news operations in a constantly more competitive marketplace," he says. But news directors on their first jobs in small markets may have lean years.

Interns

Students will continue to fill internships, usually unpaid. For most, even many who are exploited as free labor, the experience will carry educational and long-term financial benefits.

The oversupply of beginners may also mean increased use of the trainees sometimes called "super-interns." I haven't researched this, but the trade press gives an example of a TV station that hires trainees to report and shoot for one year at $5 an hour. If there's an opening when the year's up, they have an inside track. Otherwise, it's goodbye. And the station recruits someone else for a year of labor at $5 an hour.[4]

Newspapers are also using "job-hungry young journalists" as "super-interns," but at higher pay.[5]

The whole notion that working in broadcast journalism requires several months or years of "breaking-in" may be a self-serving myth created by the industry and abetted in some cases by educators. In my experience, a bright, motivated person with a solid education can be up and running quite well on most TV or radio news jobs in a matter of days or weeks, and with minimal supervision.

Minorities

It's encouraging to find that minorities in the TV news work force are being paid comparably with their white counterparts. But blacks, Hispanics, Asian Americans and American Indians remain underrepresented in broadcast news, particularly in management. TV and radio news have a long way to go just to mirror society, let alone show leadership.

"We still don't have enough diversity in our newsrooms." Georgeann Herbert, managing editor, WBBM, Chicago, says. "Too often, the minority hire is made to satisfy government requirements rather than to legitimately reflect the differing viewpoints within the community. 'Narrowcasting' may leave unenlightened owners with a good excuse to say, 'I don't need one of those.' That's an attitude that diminishes us all."

Women

Herbert is also concerned that numbers cannot "capture the subtle pressures aging women in television may feel to move into other fields or the lifestyle choices imposed on young mothers in broadcasting who no longer feel able to give up their personal lives for the news."

It's a credit to the industry that women and men generally earn comparable salaries when allowance is made for women's being younger and less experienced. Because women entered the work force late, there has been limited opportunity for age discrimination against them. But hundreds of broadcast newswomen will turn 40 in the 1990s, providing a test of whether the industry has matured regarding maturity.

Karen Foss, veteran anchorwoman at KSDK TV, St. Louis, comments, "I think it's still too soon to say if mature women will win acceptance by management and viewers in equitable numbers with their male colleagues. I certainly hope women won't be rejected for cosmetic reasons just as they acquire valuable depth and seasoning."

The fact that our population is aging can be seen as job insurance for the women who would be TV reporters and anchors of 40 and up by 2000. In my scenario, they'll be at anchor desks everywhere, not just at the networks and stations in major markets where they're concentrated today. Maturing audiences will want to see peers, female as well as male, reporting the news. These viewers will relate to wrinkles and feel comfortable with people who, like themselves, look a bit older as part of aging. Smart stations are treating their fortysomething anchorwomen with care. They'll be needed for the audiences of the 1990s, 2000 and beyond.

Talent

The major variable in the salary mix may well be talent. We're all created equal, yes, but not in ability or potential earning power.

Luck, determination, workaholism and even ingratiation may boost salaries. But the people most likely to move solidly ahead are those with talent that makes them stand out from the crowd.

Research, mine included, avoids talent as a measurable variable—it doesn't quantify easily. But it's there, normally randomized across such quantifiable variables as age and experience. Wunderkinds may skyrocket to the top in their 20s, joining the many well paid veterans who also have that something extra. At the same time, less talented workhorses plod along at low pay in all age brackets.

Broadcast news, like other fields, still needs workhorses along with thoroughbreds. But the need grows less each year. Technology is crowding them out. For automatable tasks, chips are more cost-efficient than brains. Robots are replacing studio camera operators. And a likely reason the pay for photographers is so low is that little expertise, let alone talent, is required to shoot the routine news video many stations find good enough.

Talented people will always be in demand. Even with high price tags, they're worth it. But keep in mind—they're the ones who can make it big in other fields. They may see no need to waste themselves on the unpaid internships and non-competitive entry-level pay of broadcast news.

Staff Benefits

Unless government and industry come up with some near miracles in the 1990s, a bigger portion of your salary will go to health insurance, pensions and other benefits by 2000.

Broadcast stations, like other employers, will see their profit margins go down if they continue to pay more and more into the mushrooming premiums for health insurance. So they'll keep shifting more of the burden, all in some cases, to the employee. Many small radio stations and some marginal TV stations may have no choice if they want to stay in business. Still, it amounts to a pay cut for the worker.

Under the strain of Social Security taxes, stations will

continue to pick up less of the tab for pension funds. Employees will increasingly be left to look out for their own retirement. They may find added safety in opting for plans that give them the most control over the destiny of their contributions. As reported by the news media and detailed in a book by Donald L. Barlett and James B. Steele, some corporations have been looting their pension funds, and with legal impunity.[6] They "borrow" to cover cash-flow needs that don't go away, leaving a quasi-federal agency to replenish part of the pension fund. That means part of the tax withheld from your salary goes to pay your pension contribution a second time. Some say something akin takes place when the government taxes you for Social Security, lends itself the money, then taxes you again to pay interest on the loan.

Stock options can mean a boost for long-term gains. You probably won't beat a system that puts profits ahead of people, so here's an opportunity to join it. Just beware of corporate raiders who may take your investment to bankruptcy before bailing out.

As the costs of staff benefits grow, more stations will join those that are already reducing overhead by the increased use of part-time and per diem staff. Overdone, that's exploitation.

Profits and People

One principle won't change by 2000: Profits rule the business world. And the closer you are to the money-making process, the more you can make for yourself. General managers, charged with delivering even larger profits to owners, draw their stations' highest pay. Sales managers bring in the revenue and take their cut. News directors still lag, but have moved up with the advent of newsrooms as profit centers. In the big time, stars who pull ratings outearn everybody else—box office works that way.

In fairness to owners, if broadcast profits were not reasonably competitive with those from other investments, investors would turn elsewhere and commercial broadcasting would end.

But the profit motive may be running amok. People are too often sacrificed for the greater good of profit. In the financial world, a corporation announces massive layoffs, and the price of its stock goes up—the "restructuring" promises greater profits. In broadcast news, a station underpays its reporters, photographers and producers, and overhead stays down—profits stay up. It's easy for a manager under pressure for profits to forget that the instruments of those profits are not balance sheets or robots. They're people, professionals who deserve to be paid as such.

Long-term dominance in the marketplace comes from nurturing the people who provide the news programming audiences learn to turn to. Any gains from treating staff as disposable items are short-term at best.

So, instead of asking what's the least a passable reporter will work for, many stations might well ask themselves whether profit margins need be quite so great. Is a margin of 15 percent instead of 10 percent worth the penalty in low quality and eroded audience respect that comes from a second-rate, underpaid staff? Once defected, audiences are hard to bring back.

A major infusion of salary money is overdue. Granted, some marginal stations can't pay more just now. But the resources are there in much of the industry, particularly television.[7] At hundreds of stations, it would require only a moderate shift in priorities from profits to people.

Everybody wins when staff are properly paid. Broadcast news attracts and retains talented people who turn out a news product that wins the audiences and advertisers that make profit centers of newsrooms. We tend to get what we pay for. In an ever more crowded media market, TV and radio stations that care for their people as well as profits will most likely stand out as the leaders in broadcast journalism in 2000 and beyond.

APPENDIX A

Survey Materials

UNIVERSITY OF MISSOURI-COLUMBIA

School of Journalism

Broadcast News Department

Box 838
Columbia, Missouri 65205
Telephone (314) 882-4205

June 1992

Dear News Director:

    Reliable, up-to-date information on news operations is much in demand by news directors and others. As a service to the field, RTNDA and the Radio-Television News Directors Foundation sponsor an annual survey and publish the results.

    You can help by marking and returning the enclosed questionnaire. It's fast moving -- only two pages. All responses will be confidential.

    We'll send respondents a copy of reports on average salaries, etc., calculated separately for various market sizes, including yours.

    Even if your station has no news operation, please return the questionnaire with that information marked. One thing we want to know is how many stations do not have news operations.

Sincerely,

Vernon A. Stone
Professor
Research Director, Radio-Television
    News Directors Association

Enc.

an equal opportunity institution

152 | Let's Talk Pay in Television and Radio News

TV News Survey

FOR THE PERSON IN CHARGE OF NEWS

Station _____   Market's approximate ADI rank: _____

City _____ State _____ ABC, CBS or NBC ____ Independent ____

Does your station do any locally originated news programming? Yes ____ No ____

   IF NO, skip the rest, but please return the questionnaire to let us know.

Including yourself -- and counting sports, weather and technical staff if they work primarily in the news operation -- how many employees, weekly...

   ...work 40 or more hours (or full-time) in news? ____ men ____ women

   ...work less than 40 hours (or part-time) in news? ____ men ____ women

Of all members of the news operation, including yourself, how many are?

	Black	Hispanic	American Indian	Asian American
Men	____	____	____	____
Women	____	____	____	____

Which news staff, if any, are unionized? Anchors ____ Reporters ____ Producers ____

   Photographers ____ Writers ____ Other:

How long have you worked in broadcast news? ____ years

         ...worked in news management? ____ years

  ...been in charge of this news operation? ____ years ____ months

Your age: ____ Sex: M ____ F ____

Your race: White Non-Hispanic ____ Black ____ Hispanic ____

     American Indian ____ Asian American ____

What job did you hold just before your present position?

   Old job: _____ Here? ____ Or elsewhere? ____

Do you aspire to become a station general manager? Yes ____ No ____

What is the main background of your GM? Sales ____ News ____ Program director ____

   Other:

-- OVER --

-- 2 --

Has your news operation experienced cutbacks in the past 12 months? Yes ____ No ____

   IF YES, what forms have the cutbacks taken? (Check all that apply)

   Staff layoffs ____   Reduced reporting ____

   Staff cuts through attrition ____   Reduced news airtime ____

   Reduced overtime ____   Other cutbacks:

	More Now	Less Now	About Same
How does your news airtime compare to 12 months ago?			
Morning	___	___	___
Midday	___	___	___
Early evening	___	___	___
Late evening	___	___	___
Other _____	___	___	___

In terms of paying its way at your station, does news:

   Make money? ____   Lose money? ____   Come out about even? ____

ANNUAL SALARIES of <u>full-time</u> employees (if you can't tell salary, please note range):

Typical ENG cameraperson:	$_____
Typical news producer:	$_____
Executive news producer(s):	$_____
Typical field reporter:	$_____
Typical anchorperson/newscaster:	$_____
Highest paid anchorperson/newscaster:	$_____
Assignment editor(s):	$_____
Assistant news director(s):	$_____
News director or person in charge of news:	$_____

Thank you.

154 | Let's Talk Pay in Television and Radio News

Radio News Survey

FOR THE PERSON IN CHARGE OF NEWS

Station(s) _____   Market Population: 1) Over 1 million _____
                                                   2) 250,000-1,000,000 _____
City _____ State _____   3) 50,000-250,000 _____
                                                   4) Under 50,000 _____
AM ____ FM ____ AM/FM ____ news operation

Does your station do any locally originated news programming? Yes ____ No ____

IF NO, skip the rest, but please return the questionnaire to let us know.

Including yourself -- and counting sports, weather and technical staff if they work primarily in the news operation -- how many employees, weekly...

...work 40 or more hours (or full-time) in news? ____ men ____ women

...work less than 40 hours (or part-time) in news? ____ men ____ women

Of all members of the news operation, including yourself, how many are?

	Black	Hispanic	American Indian	Asian American
Men	____	____	____	____
Women	____	____	____	____

Which news staff, if any, are unionized? Anchors ____ Reporters ____ Other:

How long have you worked in broadcast news? ____ years

　　　　　　...worked in news management? ____ years

　...been in charge of this news operation? ____ years ____ months

Your age: ____ Sex: M ____ F ____

Your race: White Non-Hispanic ____ Black ____ Hispanic ____

　　　　　American Indian ____ Asian American ____

What job did you hold just before your present position?

　　Old job: _____ Here? ____ Or elsewhere? ____

Do you aspire to become a station general manager? Yes ____ No ____

What is the main background of your GM? Sales ____ News ____ Program director ____

Other:

-- OVER --

-- 2 --

Has your news operation experienced cutbacks in the past 12 months? Yes ____ No ____

IF YES, what forms have the cutbacks taken? (Check all that apply)

Staff layoffs ____ Reduced reporting ____
Staff cuts through attrition ____ Reduced news airtime ____
Reduced overtime ____ Other cutbacks:

How does your news airtime compare to 12 months ago?	More Now	Less Now	About Same
Morning drive on AM station			
Morning drive on FM			
Afternoon drive on AM station			
Afternoon drive on FM			
Other periods on AM station			
Other periods on FM			

How does the total amount of news time compare to 12 months ago...

On AM? More now ____ Less now ____ About the same as a year ago ____

On FM? More now ____ Less now ____ About the same as a year ago ____

In terms of paying its way at your station, does news:

Make money? ____ Lose money? ____ Come out about even? ____

ANNUAL SALARIES of full-time employees (if you can't tell salary, please note range):

Typical reporter: $ _____

Typical anchorperson/newscaster: $ _____

Highest paid anchorperson/newscaster: $ _____

News director or person in charge of news: $ _____

Thank you.

TV NEWS CAREERS SURVEY

Dear Broadcast Journalist:

    Please help us in this careers survey sponsored by the Gannett Foundation and the Radio-Television News Directors Association. Questionnaires are being distributed by news directors to all news staff at a sample of stations. Results will be published and should be helpful to educators, media managers and staff. The questionnaire leaves you unidentified.

Vernon A. Stone
RTNDA Research Director

TV market rank: 1-25 ____, 26-50 ____, 51-100 ____, 101-150 ____, 151-215 ____.

News staff size: ____

Your job title: _____

How long in that position? ____ years ...at present station? ____ years

    ...in broadcast news? ____ years ...out of school? ____ years

College: None ____ Some ____ Bachelor's degree ____ Graduate degree ____

Your degree school(s) _____ Major(s) _____

What single course in college has helped you most? _____

Of courses you didn't take, which do you wish most you had? _____

In what ways did you get real-life broadcast experience while in school?

    None ____ In labs ____ Campus media ____ Paid internship ____

    Unpaid internship ____ Other:

Since school, how many times have you changed jobs? ____ ...changed cities? ____

If you were offered a much better job that required you to move to a distant city, do you think you would accept it?

    Yes ____ Likely Yes ____ Likely No ____ No ____

    IF not, why not? _____

What kind of position do you have in mind for your next job move?

What is your long-term career goal?

Appendix A | 157

What counts in your career?
For each, please rate:

	How Important to You			How Well Present Job Is Meeting Your Needs		
	Very	Fairly	Not	Very	Fairly	Not
Salary	___	___	___	___	___	___
Excitement	___	___	___	___	___	___
Challenge	___	___	___	___	___	___
Glamour	___	___	___	___	___	___
Use of your abilities	___	___	___	___	___	___
Opportunity for originality/initiative	___	___	___	___	___	___
Autonomy	___	___	___	___	___	___
Job security	___	___	___	___	___	___
Opportunity to advance	___	___	___	___	___	___
Not disruptive of personal life	___	___	___	___	___	___
Job's value to society	___	___	___	___	___	___

More about you...

Age: ____   Sex: Male ____ Female ____

Race: White ____ Black ____ Hispanic ____ American Indian ____ Asian ____

How has your race affected your career progress -- in getting a job, moving up in your field or in other ways?
                    Helped ____ Hurt ____ Made no difference ____
Comment?

How do you think your sex/gender has affected your career progress?

    Helped ____ Hurt ____ Made no difference ____ Comment?

2

158 | Let's Talk Pay in Television and Radio News

In your present job, do you supervise the work of others to the extent that you would call your job "supervisory"? Yes ____ No ____

In which of the following ways do you regularly make decisions?

    A. Make decisions on stories others cover ____
    B. On content of news programs ____
    C. On budgetary/financial matters ____
    D. On personnel hiring, position assignments or firing ____

What about the amount of responsibility you have in your position? Is it too much ____ too little ____ or about right ____?

Do you get enough performance feedback from supervisors? Yes ____ No ____

    How helpful is that feedback? Very helpful ____ So so ____ Not helpful ____

What's your annual salary? $_____

How's your salary compared to what you expected by now when you entered the field? More ____, less ____ or about the same ____?

Which best describes your overall job satisfaction?
    Very Satisfied ____ Satisfied ____ Dissatisfied ____ Very Dissatisfied ____

Have you seriously considered leaving broadcast news? Yes ____ No ____

If you got out of broadcast news, what do you think would be the main reasons?

    a. Pay ____
    b. Stress ____
    c. Family life ____
    d. Lack of advancement ____
    e. Disenchantment with field ____
    f. Racial discrimination ____
    g. Sex discrimination ____
    h. Other:

If you got out, what type of work do you think you would do?

Please give your views: Strongly Disagree   Strongly Agree

Local TV news is excelling nationally. ____ ____ ____ ____ ____

...is excelling in my station's operation. ____ ____ ____ ____ ____

I feel a sense of pride in broadcast news as a field or occupation. ____ ____ ____ ____ ____

I think I will spend the rest of my career in broadcast news or broadcast management. ____ ____ ____ ____ ____

Broadcast news courses in college are largely a waste. Best wait and learn it on the job. ____ ____ ____ ____ ____

Your job life and your personal life...

About how many hours per week do you work on your job? ____ hours

Are you married? Yes ____ No ____ Ever been divorced? Yes ____ No ____

   IF MARRIED, does your spouse have a full-time paying job? Yes ____ No ____

      Who earns more? You ____ Spouse ____

Do you have a child at home who requires care during your workday? Yes ____ No ____

   IF YES, who does most of that child care? Spouse ____ Child care center ____

      Babysitter ____ Other: _____

Have you had marital problems related to your job? Yes ____ No ____

   IF YES, please describe:

Health problems related to your job? Yes ____ No ____

   IF YES, please describe:

Other problems in personal life related to your job? Yes ____ No ____

   IF YES, please describe:

What, if anything, has most held back your career progress?

Please use the business reply envelope to return the questionnaire. If you would like a report of survey results, to be ready a few months from now, mail your name and address separately on the enclosed postcard. Your name or station will not associated with your questionnaire.

Thank you.

APPENDIX B

Television Market Size Categories

ADI 1–25

1. New York
2. Los Angeles
3. Chicago
4. Philadelphia
5. San Francisco-Oakland-San Jose
6. Boston
7. Washington
8. Dallas-Ft. Worth
9. Detroit
10. Atlanta
11. Houston
12. Cleveland
13. Minneapolis-St. Paul
14. Seattle-Tacoma
15. Miami-Ft. Lauderdale
16. Tampa-St. Petersburg
17. Pittsburgh
18. St. Louis
19. Sacramento-Stockton
20. Phoenix
21. Denver
22. Baltimore
23. Orlando-Daytona Beach
24. Hartford-New Haven
25. San Diego

Adapted from Arbitron's 1991–92 ADI (Area of Dominant Influence in descending order by number of TV households).

ADI 26–50

26. Indianapolis
27. Portland, OR
28. Milwaukee
29. Kansas City
30. Cincinnati
31. Charlotte
32. Raleigh-Durham
33. Nashville
34. Columbus, Ohio
35. Greenville-Spartansburg, SC-Ashville, NC
36. Buffalo
37. Grand Rapids-Kalamazoo-Battle Creek
38. Norfolk-Hampton-Portsmouth
39. Memphis
40. New Orleans
41. San Antonio
42. Salt Lake City
43. Providence-New Bedford
44. Oklahoma City
45. Louisville
46. West Palm Beach-Vero Beach
47. Harrisburg-York-Lancaster
48. Greensboro-Winston Salem
49. Scranton-Wilkes Barre
50. Birmingham

ADI 51–100

51. Albany-Schenectady
52. Albuquerque
53. Dayton
54. Jacksonville
55. Charleston-Huntington
56. Flint-Saginaw-Bay City
57. Little Rock
58. Tulsa
59. Fresno-Visalia
60. Richmond
61. Wichita-Hutchinson
62. Knoxville
63. Mobile-Pensacola
64. Toledo
65. Roanoke-Lynchburg
66. Syracuse
67. Green Bay-Appleton
68. Austin, TX
69. Portland-Poland Spring, ME
70. Des Moines
71. Shreveport-Texarkana
72. Rochester, NY
73. Omaha
74. Lexington
75. Paducah, KY-Marion, IL-Cape Girardeau, MO

Appendix B | 163

76. Springfield-Decatur-Champaign
77. Springfield, MO
78. Tucson
79. Las Vegas
80. Spokane
81. Chattanooga
82. Cedar Rapids-Waterloo-Dubuque
83. Davenport-Rock Island-Moline
84. Johnstown-Altoona
85. Bristol-Kingsport-Johnson City
86. South Bend-Elkhart
87. Columbia, SC
88. Huntsville-Florence
89. Jackson, MS
90. Ft. Meyers-Naples
91. Youngstown
92. Madison, WI
93. Evansville
94. Waco-Temple
95. Baton Rouge
96. Springfield, MA
97. Burlington, VT-Plattsburgh, NY
98. Lincoln-Hastings-Kearney
99. Colorado Springs-Pueblo
100. El Paso

ADI 101–150

101. Savannah
102. Ft. Wayne
103. Lansing
104. Greenville-Washington-New Bern, NC
105. Charleston, SC
106. Sioux Falls-Mitchell, SD
107. Peoria-Bloomington, IL
108. Fargo
109. Santa Barbara-San Luis Obispo
110. Montgomery-Selma
111. Salinas-Monterey
112. Augusta, GA
113. Tyler-Longview-Jacksonville
114. Brownsville-Harlingen, TX
115. Tallahassee
116. Reno
117. Eugene, OR
118. Ft. Smith, AK
119. Lafayette, LA
120. Macon, GA
121. Columbus, GA
122. Traverse City-Cadillac, MI
123. LaCrosse-Eau Claire, WI
124. Columbus-Tupelo, MS
125. Corpus Christi
126. Duluth-Superior
127. Amarillo
128. Monroe, LA-El Dorado, AR
129. Yakima, WA

130. Chico-Redding, CA
131. Wausau-Rhinelander, WI
132. Bakersfield, CA
133. Binghamton, NY
134. Birmingham
135. Beaumont-Port Arthur
136. Terre Haute
137. Sioux City
138. Florence-Myrtle Beach, SC
139. Wichita Falls, TX-Lawton, OK
140. Erie
141. Topeka
142. Boise
143. Wilmington, NC
144. Wheeling, WV-Steubenville, OH
145. Joplin, MO-Pittsburge, KS
146. Bluefield-Oak Hill, WV
147. Lubbock, TX
148. Rochester-Austin, MN-Mason City, IA
149. Medford, OR
150. Minot-Bismarck-Dickinson, ND-Glendive, MT

ADI 151–210

151. Odessa-Midland, TX
152. Columbia-Jefferson City, MO
153. Albany, GA
154. Sarasota, FL
155. Bangor, ME
156. Quincy, IL-Hannibal, MO
157. Abilene-Sweetwater, TX
158. Biloxi-Gulfport, MS
159. Clarksburg-Weston, WV
160. Idaho Falls-Pocatello
161. Utica, NY
162. Panama City, FL
163. Salisbury, MD
164. Laurel-Hattiesburg, MS
165. Gainesville, FL
166. Dothan, AL
167. Harrisonburg, VA
168. Watertown-Carthage, NY
169. Elmira, NY
170. Palm Springs, CA
171. Rapid City, SD
172. Billings-Miles City, MT
173. Alexandria, LA
174. Lake Charles, LA
175. Greenwood-Greenville, MS
176. Jonesboro, AR
177. Missoula, MT
178. Ardmore-Ada, OK
179. Grand Junction-Durango, CO
180. El Centro, CA-Yuma, AZ
181. Meredian, MS
182. Great Falls, MT
183. Jackson, TN
184. Parkersburg, WV

185. Tuscaloosa, AL
186. Marquette, MI
187. Eureka, CA
188. San Angelo, TX
189. St. Joseph, MO
190. Butte, MT
191. Bowling Green, KY
192. Hagerstown, MD
193. Lafayette, IN
194. Anniston, AL
195. Cheyenne, WY-Scottsbluff, NE-Sterling, CO
196. Charlottesville, VA
197. Casper, WY
198. Lima, OH
199. Laredo, TX
200. Twin Falls, ID
201. Ottumwa, IA-Kirksville, MO
202. Presque Isle, ME
203. Zanesville, OH
204. Mankato, MI
205. Flagstaff, AZ
206. Bend, OR
207. Victoria, TX
208. Helena, MT
209. North Platte, NE
210. Alpena, MI

APPENDIX C

Trends Tables for Middle Markets

TABLE C.1: Trend Medians for TV News Photographers

	ADI 1–25 Indies	ADI 26–50	ADI 51–100	ADI 101–150
1982	$19,500	$17,420	$12,940	$11,665
1987	$21,000 +7.7%	$20,800 +19.4%	$16,380 +26.6%	$13,350 +15.9%
1992	$29,375 +39.9%	$24,575 +18.1%	$18,475 +12.8%	$15,675 +15.9%
11-Year Change	$9,875 +50.6%	$7,155 +41.1%	$5,535 +42.8%	$4,010 +34.4%
2000 (at 87–92 avg. ann. rate)	$48,115 +63.8%	$31,700 +29.0%	$22,265 +20.5%	$19,675 +25.5%

TABLE C.2: Trend Medians for Typical TV Reporters

	ADI 1–25 Indies	ADI 26–50	ADI 51–100	ADI 101–150
1983	$21,710	$20,655	$15,625	$14,350
1987	$22,360 +3.0%	$25,000 +21.0%	$18,980 +21.5%	$15,080 +5.1%
1992	31,250 +39.8%	$30,615 +22.5%	$20,500 +8.0%	$16,900 +12.1%
9-Year Change	$9,540 +43.9%	$9,960 +48.2%	$4,875 +31.2%	$2,550 +17.8%
2000 (at 87–92 avg. ann. rate)	$51,125 +63.6%	$41,605 +35.9%	$23,125 +12.8%	$20,160 +19.3%

TABLE C.3: Trend Medians for Typical TV Producers

	ADI 1–25 Indies	ADI 26–50	ADI 51–100	ADI 101–150
1984	$24,000	$22,100	$18,200	$15,600
1987	$24,700 +2.9%	$23,920 +8.2%	$20,800 +14.3%	$15,910 +2.0%
1992	$28,750 +16.4%	$28,500 +19.1%	$21,250 +2.2%	$17,800 +11.9%
8-Year Change	$4,750 +19.8%	$6,400 +29.0%	$3,050 +16.8%	$2,200 +14.1%
2000 (at 87–92 avg. ann. rate)	$36,280 +26.2%	$37,220 +30.6%	$22,000 +3.5%	$21,180 +19.0%

TABLE C.4: Trend Medians for TV Assignment Editors

	ADI 1–25 Indies	ADI 26–50	ADI 51–100	ADI 101–150
1985	$25,100	$26,935	$23,400	$18,980
1987	$26,000 +3.6%	$27,975 +3.9%	$23,975 +2.5%	$19,970 +5.2%
1992	$32,750 +30.0%	$34,000 +21.5%	$28,035 +16.9%	$21,875 +9.5%
7-Year Change	$7,650 +30.5%	$7,065 +26.2%	$4,635 +19.8%	$2,895 +15.3%
2000 (at 87–92 avg. ann. rate)	$46,340 +41.5%	$45,730 +34.5%	$35,630 +27.1%	$25,220 +15.3%

TABLE C.5: Trend Medians for Typical TV Anchors

	ADI 1–25 Indies	ADI 26–50	ADI 51–100	ADI 101–150
1983	$30,135	$42,795	$25,780	$20,385
1987	$34,060 +13.0%	$49,975 +16.8%	$35,000 +35.8%	$24,025 +17.9%
1992	$55,000 +61.5%	$70,810 +41.7%	$39,715 +13.5%	$27,450 +12.5%
9-Year Change	$24,865 +82.5%	$28,015 +65.5%	$13,935 +54.1%	$7,065 +34.7%
2000 (at 87–92 avg. ann. rate)	$109,120 +98.4%	$118,040 +66.7%	$48,295 +21.6%	$32,940 +20.0%

TABLE C.6: Trend Medians for Typical TV Station's Highest Paid Anchor

	ADI 1–25 Indies	ADI 26–50	ADI 51–100	ADI 101–150
1982	$40,300	$48,100	$30,160	$22,800
1987	$34,100	$94,900	$51,220	$31,900
	−15.4%	+24.7%	+69.8%	+40.3%
1992	$62,500	$118,335	$58,250	$35,400
	+83.3%	+24.7%	+13.7%	+10.7%
10-Year Change	$22,220	$70,235	$28,090	$12,600
	+55.1%	+146.0%	+93.1%	+55.3%
2000 (at 87–92 avg. ann. rate)	$145,810	$165,075	$71,065	$41,455
	+133.3%	+39.5%	+22.0%	+17.1%

TABLE C.7: Trend Medians for TV Executive Producers

	ADI 1–25 Indies	ADI 26–50	ADI 51–100	ADI 101–150
1989	$33,900	$37,960	$29,950	$18,200
1992	$42,500	$41,565	$32,375	$21,875
	+25.4%	+9.5%	+8.1%	+20.2%
2000 (at 89–92 avg. ann. rate)	$71,230	$52,080	$39,370	$33,645
	+67.6%	+25.3%	+21.6%	+53.8%

TABLE C.8: Trend Medians for TV Asst. News Directors

	ADI 1–25 Indies	ADI 26–50	ADI 51–100	ADI 101–150
1988	$41,600	$40,300	$34,160	$27,455
1992	$56,500 +35.8%	$50,310 +24.8%	$35,165 +2.9%	$27,875 +1.5%
2000 (at 88–92 avg. ann. rate)	$96,955 +71.6%	$75,315 +49.7%	$37,240 +5.9%	$28,740 +3.1%

TABLE C.9: Trend Medians for TV News Directors

	ADI 1–25 Indies	ADI 26–50	ADI 51–100	ADI 101–150
1972	$17,290	$15,710	$13,910	$12,090
1977	$18,000 +4.1%	$25,870 +64.7%	$18,395 +32.2%	$15,965 +32.1%
1982	$33,800 +87.8%	$40,090 +55.0%	$30,530 +66.0%	$25,910 +62.3%
1987	$33,710 −.3%	$50,960 +27.1%	$42,120 +38.0%	$35,050 +35.3%
1992	$52,915 +57.0%	$73,250 +43.7%	$51,470 +22.2%	$34,475 +6.9%
20-Year Change	$35,625 +206.0%	$57,540 +366.3%	$37,560 +270.0%	$25,385 +210.0%
2000 (at 87–92 avg. ann. rate)	$101,175 +91.2%	$124,525 +70.0%	$69,740 +35.5%	$41,635 +11.1%

TABLE C.10: Trend Medians for Radio Reporters

	Large Markets	Medium Markets
1983	$13,000	$11,000
1987	$13,000 .0%	$11,960 +8.5%
1992	$16,400 +26.2%	$13,500 +12.9%
9-Year Change	$3,400 +26.2%	$2,500 +22.7%
2000 (at 87–92 avg. ann. rate)	$23,255 +41.8%	$16,280 +20.6%

TABLE C.11: Trend Medians for Radio Anchors

	Large Markets	Medium Markets
1983	$14,300	$11,700
1987	$15,600 +9.1%	$13,000 +11.1%
1992	$19,500 +25.0%	$16,985 +30.7%
9-Year Change	$5,200 +36.4%	$5,285 +45.2%
2000 (at 87–92 avg. ann. rate)	$27,300 +40.0%	$25,310 +49.0%

TABLE C.12: Trend Medians for Radio News Directors

	Large Markets	Medium Markets
1972	$9,100	$7,800
1977	$10,400 +14.3%	$10,400 +33.3%
1982	$18,250 +75.5%	$13,570 +30.5%
1987	$20,850 +14.2%	$15,600 +15.0%
1992	$23,150 +11.0%	$17,775 +13.9%
20-Year Change	$14,050 +154.4%	$9,975 +127.9%
2000 (at 87–92 avg. ann. rate)	$27,225 +17.6%	$21,740 +22.3%

Notes

Chapter 1.

1. **East:** Connecticut, Delaware, Maine, Maryland, Massachusetts, New Hampshire, New Jersey, New York, Pennsylvania, Rhode Island, Vermont, West Virginia, District of Columbia. **South:** Alabama, Arkansas, Florida, Georgia, Kentucky, Louisiana, Mississippi, North Carolina, South Carolina, Tennessee, Texas, Virginia. **Midwest:** Illinois, Indiana, Iowa, Kansas, Michigan, Minnesota, Missouri, Nebraska, North Dakota, Ohio, Oklahoma, South Dakota, Wisconsin. **West:** Alaska, Arizona, California, Colorado, Hawaii, Idaho, Montana, Nevada, New Mexico, Oregon, Utah, Washington, Wyoming.

2. Irving E. Fang and Frank W. Gerval, "A Survey of Salaries and Hiring Preferences in Television News," *Journal of Broadcasting* 15 (Fall 1971): 421–433.

3. John W. Johnstone, Edward J. Slawski and William W. Bowman, *The News People: A Sociological Portrait of American Journalists and Their Work.* (Urbana: University of Illinois Press, 1976), p. 235.

4. David H. Weaver and G. Cleveland Wilhoit, *The American Journalist,* 2d ed. (Bloomington: Indiana University Press, 1991), p. 84.

5. David Weaver and G. Cleveland Wilhoit, "Who Are We? A Brief

Status Report on Jobs and Work," *Quill,* Jan./Feb. 1993, pp. 45–47.

6. Conrad Smith, Eric S. Fredin and Carroll Ann Ferguson, "Sex Discrimination in Earnings and Story Assignments Among TV Reporters," *Journalism Quarterly* 65 (Spring 1988): 3–11.

7. For examples of the Kenneth Harwood's early and recent work, see his "Earnings and Education of Men and Women in Selected Media Occupations", *Journal of Broadcasting* 20 (Spring 1976): 233–237; and "Broadcasting and Cable as Employers," *Feedback* 33 (Winter 1992): 21–22.

8. Lee B. Becker, "Finding Work Was More Difficult for 1990 Grads," *Journalism Educator* 47 (Summer 1992): 65–73.

9. National Association of Broadcasters, *1992 Radio Employee Compensation and Fringe Benefits Report* (Washington: NAB, 1992); Broadcast Cable Financial Management Association and NAB, *1991 Television Employee Compensation and Fringe Benefits Report* (Washington: NAB, 1991).

Chapter 2.

1. For a more detailed report on the mostly small gains and losses in salaries from mid-1991 to mid-1992, see Vernon A. Stone, "TV News Pay Lags Cost of Living, Radio News Directors Gain," RTNDA *Communicator,* March 1993. pp. 10–12.

2. "College Students Are Paying Now for Extra Monthly Income Later," *St. Louis Post Dispatch,* Jan. 28, 1993), p. 5A.

3. An example of what even one extreme case can do to the mean: Suppose we replaced the $1 million dollar highest salary in the 1992 survey with the $3 million that Dan Rather is said to make at CBS. The mean for all TV stations' highest paid anchors increases from $90,375 to $96,345, but the median remains at $50,535. Not extreme enough? Then let's move Rather to Toledo (ADI 64) at his CBS salary. The 1992 survey's highest in ADI 51–100 markets was $150,000. Swap that for Rather's and the median for ADI 51–100 stays at $58,250, while the mean jumps from $65,290 to $95,935. The median (average star anchor's salary) remains typical, but the mean (average salary when the dollar pool is divided by the number of cases) is misleading as an indicator of what star anchors in those markets earn.

4. Sources of comparative salaries for this chapter: Edward Seaton, "Newspaper Salaries Stagnate," *ASNE Bulletin,* Nov. 1992, pp. 22–23; U.S. Department of Labor, Bureau of Labor Statistics, *Occupational Outlook Handbook* 1992–93 Edition, Bulletin 2400 (May 1992); U.S. Department of

Labor, Bureau of Labor Statistics, "White-Collar Pay in Goods-Producing Industries, March 1990," Bulletin 2374 (October 1990), pp. 66–69; U.S. Department of Labor, Bureau of Labor Statistics, "Average Hourly Earnings of Nonsupervisory Workers," *Monthly Labor Review* (September 1992), pp. 69–73; Arsen J. Darnay, ed., *American Salaries and Wages Survey* (Detroit: Gale Research Inc., 1991).

5. "U.S. Reports Poverty Hit 27-Year High," *St. Louis Post-Dispatch* Sept. 4, 1992, p. 1A.

6. Lee B. Becker and Gerald M. Kosicki, "Survey of Journalism and Mass Communications Graduates 1991," Summary Report, School of Journalism, Ohio State University, July 1992.

7. Broadcast Cable Financial Management Association (BCFM) and National Association of Broadcasters (NAB), *1991 Television Employee Compensation and Fringe Benefits Report* (Washington: NAB, 1991).

8. Becker and Kosicki, *op. cit.*

9. BCFM and NAB, *op. cit.*

Chapter 3.

1. Such specialized averages are found in Arsen J. Darnay, ed., *American Salaries and Wages Survey* (Detroit: Gale Research, 1991). The 918-page volume lists salaries, mostly local and regional, for hundreds of occupations. Other salary averages outside the mass media are from U.S. Bureau of Labor Statistics publications cited in Chapter 2.

2. "College Students Are Paying Now for Extra Monthly Income Later," *St. Louis Post-Dispatch*, Jan. 28, 1993, p. 5A.

3. Lee B. Becker and Gerald M. Kosicki, "Survey of Journalism and Mass Communications Graduates 1991," Summary Report, School of Journalism, Ohio State University, July 1992.

4. National Association of Broadcasters (NAB), *1992 Radio Employee Compensation and Fringe Benefits Report* (Washington: NAB, 1992).

5. For example, see Margaret Genovese, "Editors, Educators Lament Low Starting Salaries," *presstime*, Feb. 1985, pp. 36–37; David Hill, "Life on the Bottom Rung," *Washington Journalism Review,* Jan. 1987, pp. 20–23; Lincoln Furber, "Starting Out in the Boonies," RTNDA *Communicator,* May 1989, pp. 16–19.

Chapter 4.

1. Dan Rather with Mickey Herskowitz, *The Camera Never Blinks* (New York: Ballantine Books, 1977), p. 60.

2. Steve Weinstein, "KNBC's $8-Million Anchor," *Los Angeles Times,* July 8, 1992, pp. F1, F9.

3. Fred W. Friendly, "No Journalist Requires $1 or $2 or $3 Million a Year," *Washington Journalism Review,* May 1987, p. 20.

4. Don Hewitt, "No Journalist Requires Anything Except a Respite from Fred Friendly," *Washington Journalism Review,* May 1987, pp. 21–22.

5. Eric Mink, "Rumors Fly as CBS Gets Letterman," *St. Louis Post-Dispatch,* Jan. 15, 1993, pp. 1, 12.

6. Tom McNichol, "Mountain of Cash," *USA Weekend,* March 20, 1992, pp. 4–5.

Chapter 5.

1. Kevin Phillips, *The Politics of Rich and Poor* (New York: Random House, 1990).

2. Donald L. Barlett and James B. Steele, *America: What Went Wrong?* (Kansas City: Andrews and McMeel, 1992).

3. The national Consumer Price Index is used here, and the CPI varies by region and market size. To adjust accordingly was beyond the scope of this study.

4. Vernon A. Stone, "News Keeps Making Money," RTNDA *Communicator,* June 1992, p. 8.

5. For example, see Gary Cummings, "Lowering the Boom on Big Raises," *Washington Journalism Review,* June 1986, p. 13; Morry Roth, "ABC Stations Weigh Anchors' Pay: Don't Think Anchors Pay Way," *Variety,* July 19, 1989, p. 47; J. Max Robins, "Anchors Dropped, Jokers Yoked," *Variety,* June 24, 1991, pp. 1, 68.

Chapter 6.

1. David Weaver and G. Cleveland Wilhoit, "Who Are We? A Brief Status Report on Jobs and Work," *Quill,* Jan./Feb. 1993, pp. 45–47.

2. See, for example, John W. C. Johnstone, Edward J. Slawski and William W. Bowman, *The News People* (Urbana: University of Illinois Press, 1976), pp. 137–142; Susan Faludi, *Backlash: The Undeclared War Against American Women* (New York: Anchor/Doubleday, 1991), pp. 363–399; Sue Lafky, "Economic Equity and the Journalistic Work Force," in Pamela J. Creedon, ed., *Women in Mass Communication: Challenging Gender Values* (Newbury Park: Sage Publications, 1989), pp. 164–179.

3. Weaver and Wilhoit, *op. cit.*

4. David H. Weaver and G. Cleveland Wilhoit, *The American Journalist: A Portrait of U.S. News People and Their Work,* 2d ed. (Bloomington: Indiana University Press, 1991), pp. 82–87.

5. For example, see Lafky, *op. cit.*; Kevin Phillips, *The Politics of Rich and Poor* (New York: Random House, 1990), pp. 202–209.

6. For example, see Christine Craft, *An Anchorwoman's Story* (Santa Barbara: Capra Press, 1986); Jim Cameron, "Equal Pay for Equal Work? Not in Broadcast Journalism!" *Talkers,* Dec. 3, 1990, p. 8; Lou Prato, "Are All Anchors Created Equal?" *Washington Journalism Review,* March 1991, p. 52.

7. Faludi, *op. cit.,* p. 373.

8. Mary Ellen Schoonmaker, "TV News and the Face-Lift Factor," *Columbia Journalism Review,* March/April 1987, pp. 48–50.

9. Kate Maddox, "CBS Hit with Age, Sex Bias Complaint," *Electronic Media,* June 15, 1992, pp. 4, 42.

10. This was reported by Jill Geisler (now news director, WITI-TV, Milwaukee) in an unpublished senior thesis, "Attitudes Toward Television Newswomen," at the University of Wisconsin in 1972. Expanded research in the same ongoing project was later published in Vernon A. Stone, "Attitudes Toward Television Newswomen," *Journal of Broadcasting* 18 (Winter 1973–74): 49–62.

11. Federal Communications Commission, *Report and Order,* Docket No. 19269, RM-1722 (released Dec. 28, 1971).

Chapter 7.

1. Karl A. Idsvoog and James L. Hoyt, "Professionalism and Performance of Television Journalists," *Journal of Broadcasting* 21 (Winter 1977): 97–109.

2. Margaret H. DeFleur, "Foundations of Job Satisfaction in the Media Industries," *Journalism Educator* 47 (Spring 1992): 3–15.

3. Adam Smith, *An Inquiry into the Nature and Causes of the Wealth of the Nations,* 6th ed. (London: G. Bell and Sons, 1921), first published in 1776, p. 83 (cited in DeFleur, *ibid.*).

Chapter 8.

1. Juliet B. Schor, *The Overworked American* (New York: Basic Books, 1991), pp. 142–146.

2. Allen Freedman, "The Overtime Wars," *Columbia Journalism Review,* July/Aug. 1992, pp. 55–56; Lou Prato, "Pay Ruling Upsets Newsroom Budgets," *Washington Journalism Review,* July/Aug. 1991, p. 38.

3. Dick Meister, "What Happened to the 40-Hour Work Week?" *St. Louis Post-Dispatch,* Dec. 29, 1988, p. 3B.

4. Schor, *op. cit.,* p. 70.

5. *Ibid.,* p. 80.

6. *Ibid.,* p. 81.

Chapter 9.

1. Vernon A. Stone, "Broadcasting Market Flooded by Non-News Radio-TV Majors," *Journalism Educator* 42 (Spring 1987): 20–23.

2. TV news directors received about 60 applications for every entry-level position they filled in 1988. The ratio in radio was 24 to 1. Because the same applicant may apply to many stations, these should not be interpreted as the ratios of applicants to hires in job market. From Vernon A. Stone, "J-Grad Quality and Entry-Level Hiring Surveyed," RTNDA *Communicator,* Sept. 1989, pp. 58–59.

3. U.S. Department of Labor, "Employment Relationship Under the Fair Labor Standards Act," WH Publication 1297, quoted in J. Laurent Scharff, "Structuring Student Internships to Avoid Problems," in "Legal Notes" distributed to RTNDA members, Oct. 1992.

4. Lee B. Becker, "Survey of Journalism and Mass Communication Graduates 1990," Summary Report, School of Journalism, Ohio State University, June 1991.

5. Vernon A. Stone, "News Keeps Making Money," RTNDA *Communicator,* June 1992, p. 8.

6. For example, see "Television Bottom Line Healthy Through 1990," *Broadcasting,* Sept. 2, 1991, p. 31.

7. For example, see "Majority of Radio Stations Operating at Loss," *Broadcasting,* Aug. 26, 1991, p. 17.

8. Milan D. Meeske, "Update: Broadcast Intern Programs and Practices," *Journalism Educator* 43 (Summer 1988): 75–77.

9. Vernon A. Stone, "Broadcast News Educators and the Profession," *Journalism Quarterly* 47 (Spring 1970): 162–165.

10. Roper Organization Inc., *Electronic Media Career Preparation Study* (Washington: Radio-Television News Directors Association, Dec. 1987), pp. 51–52.

11. Robert O. Blanchard and William G. Christ, *Media Education and the Liberal Arts: A Blueprint for the New Professionalism* (Hillsdale, NJ: Lawrence Erlbaum Associates 1993), pp. 115–118.

Chapter 10.

1. Sources for the chapter's references to NAB surveys are Broadcast Cable Financial Management Association (BCFM) and National Association of Broadcasters (NAB), *1991 Television Employee Compensation and Fringe Benefits Report* (Washington: NAB, 1991); NAB, *1992 Radio Employee Compensation and Fringe Benefits Report* (Washington: NAB, 1992).

2. Vernon A. Stone and John M. Quarderer, "Staff Benefits Vary Widely," *RTNDA Communicator*, May 1988, pp. 30–33.

3. Donald L. Barlett and James B. Steele, *America: What Went Wrong?* (Kansas City: Andrews and McMeel, 1992), pp. 124–142.

4. Elizabeth Fenner, "A Lush 401(k)," *Money*, Nov. 1992, pp. 93–107.

5. Vernon A. Stone and Kimberly K. Burks, "Family Benefits in TV and Radio," RTNDA *Communicator*, Aug. 1991, pp. 24–25.

6. Personal interview with Roger D. Jett, Personnel Services, University of Missouri, Columbia, Feb. 1988.

7. Chamber of Commerce of the United States, *Employee Benefits 1983* (Washington: Chamber of Commerce of the United States, 1984).

Chapter 12.

1. Vernon A. Stone, "TV Stations Add Morning News," RTNDA *Communicator*, in press for June 1993.

2. Vernon A. Stone, "News Work Force Holds Up in TV, Drops in Radio," RTNDA *Communicator,* May 1992, pp. 18–19; Stone, "TV News Work Force Grows, Declines Continue in Radio," RTNDA *Communicator,* May 1993, pp. 26–27.

3. Vernon A. Stone, "Research Shows More News on Radio," RTNDA *Communicator,* Sept. 1992, p. 10; Stone, "Radio News Airtime Up," RTNDA *Communicator,* in press for Sept. 1993.

4. Jon Lafayette, "Station Offers Training in One-Person Setups," *Electronic Media,* Jan. 4, 1993, p. 46.

5. Kim Nauer, "The Super-Intern Saga," *Columbia Journalism Review,* Jan.-Feb. 1993, pp. 51–52.

6. Donald L. Barlett and James B. Steele, *America: What Went Wrong?* (Kansas City: Andrews and McMeel, 1992), pp. 162–188.

7. For example, see Stuart Miller, "Broadcast TV Revenues Recovered During 1992," *Variety,* March 1, 1993, p. 34.

Bibliography

Barlett, Donald L., and James B. Steele. *America: What Went Wrong?* Kansas City: Andrews and McMeel, 1992.

Becker, Lee B. "Finding Work Was More Difficult for 1990 Graduates." *Journalism Educator,* 47 (Summer 1992): 65–73.

_____. "Survey of Journalism and Mass Communication Graduates 1990." Summary Report, School of Journalism, Ohio State University, June 1991.

Becker, Lee B., and Gerald M. Kosicki. "Survey of Journalism and Mass Communications Graduates 1991." Summary Report, School of Journalism, Ohio State University, July 1992.

Blanchard, Robert O., and William G. Christ. *Media Education and the Liberal Arts: A Blueprint for the New Professionalism.* Hillsdale, NJ: Lawrence Erlbaum Associates, 1993.

Broadcast Cable Financial Management Association and National

Association of Broadcasters. *1991 Television Employee Compensation and Fringe Benefits Report*. Washington: National Association of Broadcasters, 1991.

Broadcasting & Cable Marketplace. New Providence, NJ: R.R. Bowker, of Reed Reference Publishing Co., 1992.

Cameron, Jim. "Equal Pay for Equal Work? Not in Broadcast Journalism!" *Talkers,* Dec. 3, 1990, p. 8.

Chamber of Commerce of the United States. *Employee Benefits 1983*. Washington: Chamber of Commerce of the United States, 1984.

Craft, Christine. *An Anchorwoman's Story.* Santa Barbara: Capra Press, 1986.

"College Students Are Paying Now for Extra Monthly Income Later." *St. Louis Post-Dispatch,* Jan. 28, 1993, p. 5A.

Cummings, Gary. "Lowering the Boom on Big Raises." *Washington Journalism Review,* June 1986, p. 13.

Darnay, Arsen J., ed. *American Salaries and Wages Survey.* Detroit: Gale Research Inc., 1991.

DeFleur, Margaret H. "Foundations of Job Satisfaction in the Media Industries." *Journalism Educator* 47 (Spring 1992): 3–15.

Faludi, Susan. *Backlash: The Undeclared War Against American Women.* New York: Anchor/Doubleday, 1991.

Fang, Irving E., and Frank W. Gerval. "A Survey of Salaries and Hiring Preferences in Television News." *Journal of Broadcasting* 15 (Fall 1971): 421–433.

Federal Communications Commission. *Report and Order.* Docket No. 19269, RM-1722 (released Dec. 28, 1971).

Fenner, Elizabeth. ""A Lush 401(k)." *Money,* Nov. 1992, pp. 93–107.

Freedman, Allen. "The Overtime Wars." *Columbia Journalism Review,* July/Aug. 1992, pp. 55–56.

Friendly, Fred W. "No Journalist Requires $1 or $2 or $3 Million a Year." *Washington Journalism Review,* May 1987, p. 20.

Furber, Lincoln. "Starting Out in the Boonies." RTNDA *Communicator,* May 1989, pp. 16–19.

Geisler, Jill. "Attitudes Toward Television Newswomen." Senior thesis, University of Wisconsin, 1972.

Geovese, Margaret. "Editors, Educators Lament Low Starting Salaries." *presstime,* Feb. 1985, pp. 36–37.

Harwood, Kenneth. "Broadcasting and Cable as Employers." *Feedback* 33 (Winter 1992): 21–22.

_____. "Earnings and Education of Men and Women in Selected Media Occupations." *Journal of Broadcasting* 20 (Spring 1976): 233–237.

Hewitt, Don. "No Journalist Requires Anything Except a Respite from Fred Friendly." *Washington Journalism Review,* May 1987, pp. 21–22.

Hill, David. "Life on the Bottom Rung." *Washington Journalism Review,* Jan. 1987, pp. 20–23.

Isdsvoog, Karl A., and James L. Hoyt. "Professionalism and Performance of Television Journalists." *Journal of Broadcasting* 21 (Winter 1977): 97–109.

Jett, Roger D. Personal interview by John M. Quarderer at Personnel Services, University of Missouri, Columbia, Feb. 1988.

Johnstone, John W., Edward J. Slawski and William W. Bowman. *The News People: A Sociological Portrait of American Journalists and Their Work.* Urbana: University of Illinois Press, 1976.

Lafayette, Jon. "Station Offers Training in One-Person Setups." *Electronic Media,* Jan. 4, 1993, p. 46.

Lafky, Sue. "Economic Equity and the Journalistic Work Force." In Pamela J. Creedon, ed., *Women in Mass Communication: Challenging Gender Values.* Newbury Park: Sage Publications, 1989.

Maddox, Kate. "CBS Hit with Age, Sex Bias Complaint." *Electronic Media,* June 15, 1992, pp. 4,42.

"Majority of Radio Stations Operating at Loss." *Broadcasting,* Aug. 26, 1991, p. 17.

McNichol, Tom. "Mountain of Cash." *USA Weekend*, March 20, 1992, pp. 4–5.

Meeske, Milan D. "Update: Broadcast Intern Programs and Practices." *Journalism Educator* 43 (Summer 1988): 75–77.

Meister, Dick. "What Happened to the 40-Hour Work Week?" *St. Louis Post-Dispatch,* Dec. 29, 1988, p. 3B.

Miller, Stuart. "Broadcast TV Revenues Recovered During 1992." *Variety,* March 1, 1993, p. 34.

Mink, Eric. "Rumors Fly as CBS Gets Letterman." *St. Louis Post-Dispatch,* Jan. 15, 1993, pp. 1, 12.

National Association of Broadcasters. *1992 Radio Employee Compensation and Fringe Benefits Report.* Washington: National Association of Broadcasters, 1992.

Nauer, Kim. "The Super-Intern Saga." *Columbia Journalism Review,* Jan.-Feb. 1993, pp. 51–52.

Phillips, Kevin. *The Politics of Rich and Poor.* New York: Random House, 1990.

Prato, Lou. "Are All Anchors Created Equal?" *Washington Journalism Review,* March 1991, p. 52.

———. "Pay Ruling Upsets Newsroom Budgets." *Washington Journalism Review,* July/Aug. 1991, p. 38.

Rather, Dan, with Mickey Herskowitz. *The Camera Never Blinks.* New York: Ballantine Books, 1977.

Robins, J. Max. "Anchors Dropped, Jokers Yoked." *Variety,* June 24, 1991, pp. 1, 68.

Roper Organization Inc. *Electronic Media Career Preparation Study.* Washington: Radio-Television News Directors Association, Dec. 1987, pp. 51–52.

Roth, Morry. "ABC Stations Weigh Anchors' Pay: Don't Think Anchors Pay Way." *Variety,* July 19, 1989, p. 47.

Seaton, Edward. "Newspaper Salaries Stagnate." *ASNE Bulletin,* Nov. 1992, pp. 22–23.

Schoonmaker, Mary Ellen. "TV News and the Face-Lift Factor." *Columbia Journalism Review,* March/April 1987, pp. 48–50.

Schor, Juliet B. *The Overworked American.* New York: Basic Books, 1991.

Smith, Adam. *An Inquiry into the Nature and Causes of the Wealth of the Nations.*, 6th ed. London: G. Bell and Sons, 1921. First published in 1776. Cited in Margaret H. DeFleur. "Foundations of Job Satisfaction in the Media Industries."

Journalism Educator 47 (Spring 1992): 3–15.

Smith, Conrad, Eric S. Fredin and Carroll Ann Ferguson. "Sex Discrimination in Earnings and Story Assignments Among TV Reporters." *Journalism Quarterly* 65 (Spring 1988): 3–11.

Stone, Vernon A. "Attitudes Toward Television Newswomen." *Journal of Broadcasting* 18 (Winter 1973–74): 49–62.

_____. "Broadcast News Educators and the Profession." *Journalism Quarterly* 47 (Spring 1970): 162–165.

_____. "Broadcasting Market Flooded by Non-News Radio-TV Majors." *Journalism Educator* 42 (Spring 1987): 20–23.

_____. "J-Grad Quality and Entry-Level Hiring Surveyed." RTNDA *Communicator,* Sept. 1989, pp. 58–59.

_____. "News Keeps Making Money." RTNDA *Communicator,* June 1992, p. 8.

_____. "News Work Force Holds Up in TV, Drops in Radio." RTNDA *Communicator,* May 1992, pp. 18–19.

_____. "Radio News Airtime Up." RTNDA *Communicator,* in press for Sept. 1993.

_____. "Research Shows More News on Radio." RTNDA *Communicator,* Sept. 1992, p. 10.

_____. "TV News Pay Lags Cost of Living, Radio News Directors Gain." RTNDA *Communicator,* March 1993, pp. 10–12.

_____. "TV News Work Force Grows, Declines Continue in Radio." RTNDA *Communicator,* May 1993, pp. 26–27.

———. "TV Stations Add Morning News." RTNDA *Communicator,* in press for June 1993.

Stone, Vernon A., and Kimberly K. Burks. "Family Benefits in TV and Radio." RTNDA *Communicator,* Aug. 1991, pp. 24–25.

Stone, Vernon A., and John M. Quarderer. "Staff Benefits Vary Widely." RTNDA *Communicator,* May 1988, pp. 30–33.

"Television Bottom Line Healthy Through 1990." *Broadcasting,* Sept. 2, 1991, p. 31.

U.S. Department of Labor. "Employment Relationship Under the Fair Labor Standards Act." WH Publication 1297 Quoted in J. Laurent Scharff, "Structuring Student Internships to Avoid Problems." Unpublished *Legal Notes* distributed to RTNDA members, Oct. 1992.

U.S. Department of Labor, Bureau of Labor Statistics. "Average Hourly Earnings of Nonsupervisory Workers." *Monthly Labor Review* (September 1992), pp. 69–73.

———. *Occupational Outlook Handbook 1992–93 Edition.* Bulletin 2400 (May 1992).

———. "White-Collar Pay in Goods-Producing Industries, March 1990." Bulletin 2374 (October 1990).

"U.S. Reports Poverty Hit 27-Year High." *St. Louis Post-Dispatch,* Sept. 4, 1992, p. 1A.

Weaver, David H., and G. Cleveland Wilhoit. *The American Journalist,* 2d ed. Bloomington: Indiana University Press, 1991.

———. "Who Are We? A Brief Status Report on Jobs and Work." *Quill,* Jan./Feb. 1993, pp. 45–47.

Weinstein, Steve. "KNBC's $8-Million Anchor." *Los Angeles Times,* July 8, 1992, pp. F1, F9.

Index

ABC, 8, 46, 142
Address, 5
Age discrimination, 80-81
Anchors, 66-67, 94
    fortysomething women as, 80-81
    future pay of, 144
    highest paid, 2, 22, 44-45, 61-62
    male and female, 78-79
    news, 23
    radio, 32-33, 49-50, 95, 172
    sports, 23
    star, 22, 44-46, 61-62, 170, 176
    typical, 20-21, 44, 59-61, 169
    weather, 23-24
Arbitron ADI (Area of Dominant Influence), 7
Assignment editors, 19-20, 40, 59, 94, 169
Assistant general manager, 28
Assistant news directors, 25-26, 47, 63, 94, 171

Barlett, Donald L., 54, 148
Becker, Lee, 27, 36, 11, 107
Benefits, 111-12
    assessing, 124
    bonuses, 118
    dental insurance, 114-15
    dependents medical insurance, 113-14
    employee medical insurance, 112, 113
    family, 121-24
    future, 147-48
    life insurance, 115-16
    maternity, 121-22
    package examples, 119-20
    profit-sharing plans, 118
    retirement/pension plans, 116-17
Bonuses, 10, 118
Bowman, William W., 11
Broadcasting & Cable Market Place, 5
Broadcasting Yearbook, 5
"Broadcast News," 2
Brokaw, Tom, 46
Burks, Kimberly K., 121
Business reply envelopes, 5, 6
Buying power, 9

Careers surveys, 6-7
CBS, 8, 45-46, 176
Census Bureau, 9, 13
Chamber of Commerce, 124
Chief engineer, 29, 37-38
Child care, 124-24
College education, 100-103, 126-28
Communicator, 3
Consumer Price Index-Urban, 9, 13
Cost of living, 9

Dental insurance, 114-15
Dow Jones Newspaper Fund, 11

Employee Assistance Programs, 123
Engleman, Tom, 11
Entry-level jobs, 27-28, 35-36, 180

Executive producers, 24-25, 46-47, 62-63, 94, 170

Fair Labor Standards Act of 1938, 92, 97, 105-6
Family benefits, 121-24
Fang, Irving E., 11
Federal Family and Medical Leave Act of 1993, 123-24
Ferguson, Carroll Ann, 11
Foss, Karen, 146
Frank N. Magid Associates, 112
Fredin, Eric, 11
Freedom Forum, 6, 7, 74, 104, 157-60
Friendly, Fred, 45

Geisler, Jill, 179
General manager, 28-29, 36, 144
General sales manager, 28-29, 36
Gerval, Frank W., 11
Giles, Lee, 29-30, 142, 143, 144

Hall, Lee, 142
Hanson, Gary, 140, 143
Harwood, Kenneth, 11
Health insurance, 10
Heckman, Fred, 3
Herbert, Georgeann, 32-33, 34, 145-46
Hewitt, Don, 45-46

Iacocca, Lee, 46
Independent stations, 8, 15-16, 21
Indiana University, 11
Interns, 99-109, 144-45

Jennings, Peter, 46
Job satisfaction, 129-35
Johnstone, John W.C., 11

KDFW-TV, 92
KNBC, 45
Kosicki, Gerald, 27, 36
KSDK-TV, 106, 146

Labor Department, 9, 11
Letterman, David, 46

Liberal arts education, 128-29
Life insurance, 10, 115-16

McMahon, Ed, 5
Madonna, 46
Mailings, 5-6
Managing editors, 94
Market size, 7-8, 161-65
Maternity benefits, 121-22
Mean vs. median, 14, 176
Median salary, 13-14
Medical insurance
  dependents, 113-14
  employee, 112, 113
Meister, Dick, 97
Minorities, 69-71, 87
  future pay, 145
  internships and, 104
  top-paid jobs, 127
Moyer, Paul, 45

National Association of Broadcasters surveys, 11-12, 27-29, 36, 111-14
NBC, 8, 46
Network affiliated stations, 15-16, 21
Newscasters, 32-33
News directors
  male/female, 74-78
  radio, 35, 95, 50-51, 67-68, 139-40, 173
  surveys, 3-5
  television, 26-27, 29, 48, 63-65, 94, 138-39, 171
Newspaper comparisons, 16, 17, 19, 24, 27-28, 107-108
Newsroom managers, 24-27, 46-48, 62-65
News staff careers surveys, 6-7, 70-74, 78, 84, 104, 125
Nicholson, Jack, 2

Ohio State University, 11, 27, 107
Operations directors, 36
Overtime, 91-92
  overwork, 97-98

part of salary budget, 96
pay, 10
in radio, 94-95
in television, 92-94

Pension plans, 10, 116-17
Phillips, Kevin, 54
Photographers, 15-16, 29, 40-41, 55-56, 92-93, 144, 167
Poverty level (1991), 17
Producers, 168
Producers, 18-19, 40-41, 58, 93-94, 168
Profits, 148-49
Profit-sharing plans, 10, 118
Program manager, 29, 36
Projections for 2000, 54
radio, 65-68
television, 55-65
Quarderer, John, 112

Radio averages
anchors/newscasters, 32-33
around station, 36-37
benefits examples, 120
forecasts, 139-40
news directors, 35, 36, 77-78
overtime, 94-95
reporters, 31-32
salary ranges, 49-51
salary satisfaction, 86-87, 89-90
sportscasters, 34
station categories, 7
trends, 65-68
Rather, Dan, 39, 46, 176
Regional breaks, 9
Reporters
radio, 31-32, 49, 65-66, 95, 172
television, 16-18, 40-41, 56-57, 93, 144
Research, by others, 10-12, 28-29, 71, 74, 83-84, 107-109, 111-18
Retirement plans, 116-17
Rooney, Emily, 142
Roosevelt, Franklin D., 97
Roper Organization, 108

RTNDA surveys, 3, 6-7, 74, 92, 112, 152-56
Salary
bottom and top, 125-29
ranges, 39-40
basic journalists, 40-41
newsroom managers, 46-48
radio, 49-51
satisfaction, 83-84
radio, 86-87, 89-90
television, 84-86, 87-89
surveys, 3
Sanders, Marlene, 79
Schor, Juliet B., 97-98
"Sixty Minutes," 45-46
Slawski, Edward J., 11
Smith, Conrad, 11
Social studies, 128-29
Sports anchor, 23
Sportscasters, 34
Staff size, 8-9
Star anchor, 22, 44-46, 61-62
Station manager, 28
Steele, James B., 54, 148
Stress, 130
"The Sunshine Gospel Hour," 91
Survey
materials, 151-60
procedures
careers, 6-7
market size, 7-8
news director, 3-5
staff size, 8-9
U.S. areas, 9
response rates, 4

Talent, 146-47
Television averages
anchors, 20-24
around station, 28-30
benefits examples, 119
basic journalists, 14-20
entry level, 27-28
forecasts, 138-39, 141-42
male/female
anchors, 78-81

news directors, 74-76
market size categories, 161-65
newsroom managers, 24-27
overtime, 92-94
salary ranges, 39-48
salary satisfaction, 84-86, 87-89
station, categorizing, 7-8
top and bottom salaries, 125-29
why median, 13-14
Trends, 53-54
basic journalists, 55-59
middle markets tables, 167-73
Tyson, Mike, 46

University of Houston, 11
University of Illinois at Chicago, 11
University of Minnesota, 11
University of Missouri, 112, 124
University of Wisconsin-Madison, 100, 106

Villasana, Tony, 106-7

WBBM, 30, 145
Weathercaster, 23-24
Weaver, David H., 11
WHAS-TV, 91
WHBQ-TV, 121
Wilhoit, G. Cleveland, 11
Winfrey, Oprah, 46
WISH-TV, 30, 142, 143, 144
WITI-TV, 179
WKAY, 91
WKBN-TV, 140, 143
Women, 69-74, 87
  attitudes toward, 179
  in entry-level jobs, 127
  future pay for, 146
  internships and, 104
Workaholism, 97-98
"World News Tonight," 142
Writing courses, 128-29
WSB Radio, 142
WTMJ-TV and Radio, 106

About the Author

Vernon A. Stone is a journalism professor emeritus at the University of Missouri, Columbia, and research director for the Radio-Television News Directors Association (RTNDA), which has sponsored his annual surveys on salaries and other topics since 1972. He has also conducted research under grants from the National Science Foundation, the National Association of Broadcasters and the Freedom Forum.

He is the author or co-author of more than 150 research articles and convention papers on communication effects and broadcast news, a book on television news techniques, and an RTNDA careers booklet that's in its 7th edition.

His academic career was preceded by nine years at WHAS TV and radio, Louisville, where he worked in all aspects of broadcast news—reporter, anchor, photographer, newsfilm editor, producer and TV news coordinator (sometimes all in the same day).

He left the newsroom to earn a Ph.D. at the University of Wisconsin, Madison, where he remained as a faculty member to head the broadcast news program for several years. He later served as director of the School of Journalism at Southern Illinois University, Carbondale.

Dr. Stone is a recipient of RTNDA's John F. Hogan Distinguished Service Award.

Books and Audio Cassettes for Broadcasters

How to Read Copy
Professionals' Guide to Delivering Voice-Overs and Broadcast Commercials
Adrian Cronauer

A book for both professional announcers and aspiring broadcasters. The goal is straightforward: To help announcers sound natural on the air (a 25-minute audio cassette produced by Cronauer included FREE with the book).

ISBN 0-929387-14-7, clothbound, 200 pp., $29.95

Broadcast Voice Handbook
How to Polish Your On-Air Delivery
(co-published with the RTNDA)
Ann S. Utterback, Ph.D.

The book begins with the production of the breath and moves through producing and resonating sound waves, to the articulation of sound, and, finally, the methods of stressing meaning.

ISBN 0-929387-16-3, clothbound, 264 pp., $26.95

Audio Cassettes
Vocal Expressiveness

Dr. Ann S. Utterback explains two methods to use to bring news stories to life: script making and an interpersonal communication approach.

Vocal Exercises

Dr. Utterback leads you step-by-step through exercises and drills to improve breathing, increase resonance, and polish articulation.

Coping with Stress

Dr. Utterback talks about stress—what it is, how it affects the body and the voice, and ways to begin to stress-proof your life. Side two offers a series of relaxation techniques including a guided relaxation period.

All audiocassettes co-produced with the RTNDA, $19.95

Writing Broadcast News
Shorter, Sharper, Stronger
Mervin Block

Hundreds of examples from local and network news, radio and TV—with rewrites and commentary.

ISBN 0-933893-20-5, clothbound, 231 pp., $24.95

Rewriting Network News
WorthWatching Tips from 345 TV and Radio Scripts
Mervin Block

Rewriting Network News showcases mistakes, network mistakes. These examples, plus corrections and revisions, show how to write more effective broadcast copy.

ISBN 0-929387-15-5, clothbound, 220 pp., $24.95

PN 4888 .B74 S76 1993